THE BOOK OF DUENDE

ALSO BY JASON WEBSTER

Duende: A Journey in Search of Flamenco

Andalus: Unlocking the Secrets of Moorish Spain

¡Guerra! Living in the Shadows of the Spanish Civil War

Sacred Sierra: A Year on a Spanish Mountain

*The Spy with 29 Names (*Published in the U.S. as *The Great Garbo Deception: Hitler, D-Day and a Man Called Juan)*

*Violencia: A New History of Spain (*Published in the U.S. as *Why Spain Matters: A History of the Land that Shaped the Western World)*

THE MAX CÁMARA CRIME NOVELS

Or the Bull Kills You

A Death in Valencia

The Anarchist Detective

Blood Med

A Body in Barcelona

Fatal Sunset

MOSAICS OF SPAIN SERIES

Volume I: The World of Max Cámara

Volume II: The Art of Flamenco

SCREENPLAY

The Great Garbo Deception

THE BOOK OF DUENDE

JASON WEBSTER

CORSARIO

CORSARIO

www.corsariobooks.com
info@corsariobooks.com

First published by Corsario, 2022

THE BOOK OF DUENDE

Copyright © Jason Webster

www.jasonwebster.net

The right of Jason Webster to be identified
as the owner of this work has been asserted by them in accordance
with the Copyright, Designs and Patents Act 1988.

ISBN: 978-1-913955-09-0

All rights reserved
Copyright throughout the world

No part of this publication may be reproduced or transmitted in any form or by any means, electronic, mechanical or photographic, by recording or any information storage or retrieval system or method now known or to be invented or adapted, without prior permission obtained in writing from the publisher, Corsario Books, except by a reviewer quoting brief passages in a review written for inclusion in a journal, magazine, newspaper, blog or broadcast.

For Salud, Arturo and Gabi

Every experience of duende is a whisper from the other side.

Rosario Blanco

CONTENTS

Preface — xiii

THE SUMMONS — 1

THE GATHERING — 5

THE SONG OF THE AIR — 13

DUENDE AND DJINN — 17

FOUR STORIES — 31

PROVERBS I — 57

ON DUENDE I — 65

SILVER COWBELLS — 73

WISDOM OF OLD GRANADA I — 77

TWO GRANADAN WRITERS — 83

VIEWPOINTS — 91

TWO LYRICS — 103

WISDOM OF OLD GRANADA II — 109

ON DUENDE II — 115

THREE STORIES — 121

TEN POEMS — 145

PROVERBS II — 169

BEING AND CONNECTION	175
ON DUENDE III	179
WISDOM OF OLD GRANADA III	187
THREE STORIES	193
ON DUENDE IV	215
Epilogue	221
Acknowledgments	227
Request	229

PREFACE

Imagine an energy, a concept, a supra-natural force, and a possibility which is both exclusive to a specific culture and geographical area, yet which has a universality that crosses all boundaries of language, place and belief.

To this paradox would have to be added the assertion that this 'power' has existed within a limited period – roughly the past two hundred years – while simultaneously belonging to a dimension that is essentially outside chronological time as it is ordinarily conceived.

As if this weren't enough, the matter under consideration can only be perceived, apparently, through a direct experience which may include the normal five senses as we know them, but which also seems to require another 'sense' that cannot easily be described and which may or may not be possessed by all.

Such a seemingly impossible combination of factors into one concept might easily be dismissed out of hand were it not for the fact that at various times it has been taken very seriously by great minds and thinkers. Goethe, in the 19th century, and later Lorca, in the 20th, both wrote about it with reverence, while painters, pilgrims and poets have all referred to its importance in their tasks. Actor Andy García has spoken about it in relation to his film work; the American mezzo-soprano Carla Dirlikov Canales has made a successful Internet talk about it that has been seen by thousands around the world; and Australian singer-songwriter Nick Cave states categorically that 'all love songs' must have it.

Duende, as this subtlety is called, is one of the most powerful, but also most personal, experiences any of us can have. Which is why it can almost never be defined. It can speak of joy, grief, ecstasy, emptiness, solitude, oneness – all manner of feelings, often several at once.

In a flamenco context, duende encapsulates the moment in a performance when, inexplicably, your hair stands on end, something disturbing and magnificent seems to stir in your blood, and you have the feeling – a whisper, only partially heard – of the existence of worlds beyond worlds.

The experience may be fleeting, gone almost as

soon as it is registered. Or it may be sustained. But how long it lasts is of little importance for, in essence, a single, concentrated point of duende may take years to digest, can – and frequently does – cause significant change in people's lives. I have seen men rip their shirts open with near madness and grief because of it, while others sat in total silence, motionless, heads bowed as though in communion. It can be as disturbing as it is vivifying, can speak as much of 'distance' as of 'presence'.

Twenty years after my first book, *Duende: A Journey in Search of Flamenco* was published, I am returning to the subject that was always the beating heart of that story: not the adventures and brushes with death, not even the flamenco, but the mysterious spirit around which it is built – duende itself.

The concept has become closely associated with flamenco, and for many is almost synonymous with it. But duende, in fact, exists outside the art form, and has a reality and tradition dating back many centuries, with roots stretching far beyond Andalusia. Injected over a thousand years ago into Iberian culture (where it found fertile ground) it is a universal truth: subtle, powerful and essential, and with an important message not just for Spaniards, but for people all over the world.

The result is this, *The Book of Duende*, a work which separates the essence (duende) from the vehicle (flamenco) and lays it bare, liberating it from the culture with which it has been inextricably linked since the early 19th century and placing it in the hands of everyone and anyone, no matter their origin or background, and with no interest in flamenco or even Spain necessary as an entry key.

As a collection of essays, aphorisms, poems, proverbs, lyrics and folk tales, it is designed to create a multiple, kaleidoscopic impact that is simultaneously whole and complete – not unlike duende itself. And as with duende, it can be absorbed in a single sitting, or dipped into over time. My hope is that it will help lead to a deeper understanding of an energy and potential that has been at the core of my life, even if I didn't always have a word for it, for as long as I can remember.

For the past two hundred years, Spanish art forms have effectively acted as guardians of duende, nurturing it while also being nurtured by it, keeping it alive and giving it a means through which to communicate its secrets to those capable of hearing them.

Today, however, I believe duende can be spoken of in its pure form: nothing less than a living element necessary for a greater understanding of ourselves and our destiny.

April 2022, Valencia

THE SUMMONS

THE SUMMONS

They're summoning me now;
I can hear their keys rattle,
As my heart weeps
Blood.

I'm selling all my clothes
To whoever will take them:
It's all that I have
To buy your freedom.

I cry to the moon
White tear in the sky,
Beg my father's release
From his dark prison cell.

What voices are those
Still calling my name?
My mother is broken,
Seeks me high and low.

We are the persecuted
And like dogs we flee,
Misery and hunger
Clawing our insides.

When the judge called my name,
It chilled my spine.
How full was the courtroom!
How empty the world!

The doors opened in
And a voice rang out:
So began the hearing
Of a sentence to death.

— Traditional Andalusian

THE GATHERING

THE GATHERING

Twelve people sit in a loosely defined circle in a small room at the centre of stone building perched on the northern slope of a hill. The room is a structure within a structure: it has no external walls, no windows, and only a single door of pitch pine which communicates with the rest of the house. The ceiling is constructed of rough beams of cypress running east to west, with arched earthenware tiles channelling between them. The floor is made of a combination of bare limestone flags, partially worn through centuries of footfall, which frame an inner square made of unvarnished terracotta slabs. The walls are unadorned and plastered thick with an annual application of whitewash.

On the northern side of the room, towards the

eastern corner, there is a fireplace raised two feet off the ground with a masonry smoke hood. A blackened iron grate holds the glowing embers of pine and holm oak logs which were lit hours before using the dried peel of an orange as a firelighter. The smell of smoke, penetrating every inch of the airless enclosed space, is combined with the mustiness of red wine where it has spilled and soaked into the porous floor, along with tobacco and the damp heat of bodies and breath.

The twelve people present are all known to one another: to be here is a special privilege, an honour, a sign of belonging to an exclusive group. On rare occasions, outsiders are invited to join – strictly as observers, not participants, and on the understanding that it is unlikely they will ever be invited again.

In order to take part in the ceremony that is about to occur, it is assumed that, as a minimum, everyone present is equipped with a particular faculty of perception necessary to appreciate what is about to happen. This is not a 'sense' in the ordinary meaning of the word, but something more subtle, invisible to the eye and unknown to contemporary science. It is never spoken of among those present – to do so would be unthinkable. Yet each one is aware of it and its functioning, and of its being a prerequisite for entry to this room.

Even to know about the room, to be shown it, is

considered unusual. The majority of visitors – when they have them – are taken to the rest of the building, areas open to public viewing. Much like a harem in a traditional Muslim household, this space is reserved for a very select few, and although no one would use the word – because words often have too many and not always appropriate associations – there is something of the sacred about it: secret and essential.

There is a calm and natural hierarchy within the group and each person understands their role and position within it. Opposite the door, at the eastern end, sits woman in her late 60s. She has black hair, starting to grey, parted in the middle and pulled back into a loose bun. She wears thick black eyeliner and long golden earrings which almost touch her shoulders. A black silk shawl embroidered with rose patterns in vibrant colours is draped around her upper arms and clasped by a bright-green gemstone brooch at the centre of her breast. Although there is no light shining directly on her, she seems illuminated, a glow within her eyes as she welcomes each person present, with an air of anticipation, of hope and expectancy.

To her right there is a much older man dressed in a dark grey suit with a white shirt and navy tie. He is clean-shaven and his thin white hair is combed back with brilliantine over a bronzed head, deeply lined and patched with liver spots like a dervish cloak. His back is arched with age and his chin rests close to his chest as he sits in silence, both hands clasped over the curved handle of the walking stick that stands perpendicular between his knees, looking to anyone who might not know him as though he were alone. Yet the woman, and everyone else, is acutely aware of his presence, almost as though this gathering and what is about to take place were solely for his benefit. He looks, to all intents and purposes, like a long-retired bank clerk or a medium-ranking state functionary, existing in moderate comfort on a just-adequate pension – and indeed he may well be. Yet a single adornment in his attire, a heavy yet elegant gold chain embedded with amulets and draped over his gnarled left wrist, signals that there is something extraordinary about him, that he knows something important, has had experiences that in some way set him apart.

To the right of the woman, forming the final element in a trio at the top of the room, sits a second man in his mid-forties wearing a light-blue shirt open at the collar and dark-grey trousers. He is slim and fit and his eyes are sombre and penetrating, as though he might read the secret thoughts of anyone present should he so wish. He sports a closely cropped beard fashioned into a point on his chin, which adds an intense seriousness to his expression, like a cross between a devil and a saint. His right leg is draped horizontally over his left as he leans forwards and places a final log on the fire. Everyone understands that this is the sign to begin, and the others present, sitting with their backs to the walls, finish their conversations and turn to participate.

The woman strokes her hands over her knees as though to straighten her skirt, and casts her eyes to the floor. Then, after a moment's silence, she closes them, breathes in deeply through her nose, holds for a second, and breathes out.

On cue, the old man to her right lifts his walking stick almost imperceptibly from the floor, barely seeming to move at all, and brings the point down on to the flagstone below with a hard clean *TOK*. He does this three times in succession, followed by two more beats delivered at a slower rhythm, alternating between the three and the two with an effortless precision.

The woman is concentrating on the echoing sound, and her expression, previously calm and smiling, has become knotted with acute emotion, lips tight, brow furled, as she simultaneously searches both within herself and in the atmosphere of the room for the active ingredient that she needs in order to begin. As she does so, she starts a low hum, parting her lips slightly so that the sound may be heard, yet as though singing inwardly, in towards herself, down into her chest, seeking a resonance between the cavity of her own upper body and the chamber in which they are sitting.

Finally, like one finding and grasping a key needed to open a door, she lifts her head, opens her mouth wider, and with eyes still tightly closed, begins to chant.

THE SONG OF THE AIR

THE SONG OF THE AIR

*I climbed the city walls,
Heard the wind in reply:
'Why do you weep
Now that all hope has gone?'*

*But the air itself cried
When it saw the deep wounds
Cut hard in my breast.*

*I fell in love with the air,
The air of a woman.
And as woman is air,
In the air I remained.*

I envy the air
That brushes your face.
Were that air another man,
I would kill him.

— Traditional Andalusian

DUENDE AND DJINN

DUENDE AND DJINN

Encyclopaedias and dictionaries will tell you that the word 'duende' has its origins in the Spanish phrase *dueño de casa*, literally 'master of the house', a term to describe invisible spirits who were believed to exist within a building, either protecting it or playing mischief with its human occupants depending on their nature. According to etymologists, the first two words of the phrase were elided and joined to form *duende*.

Etymology is not always an exact science, however, and sometimes finds itself at the mercy of intellectual fashion and trends. In Spain, for example, multiple attempts have been made – with only partial success – to cleanse the culture of Arabic and Jewish influences absorbed during the 900 years when Islamic civilisation was present on the Iberian Peninsula. In the late 19th century this tendency took the form of a campaign by numerous writers to stamp out Arabic loanwords in the language in favour of Latin-based equivalents, convinced that the country's Moorish heritage, far from being something to be proud of, was in fact the cause of Spain's perceived backwardness at the time in comparison with her northern European neighbours.

As a result, a distinct anti-Arab bias has grown up in the general Spanish view of the origin of many words its speakers use on a daily basis. An average (and frequently Catholic) Spaniard or Latin American, for example, is usually unaware that the name of the God of Islam, Allah, passes their lips every time they express desire (*ojalá*), surprise (*¡hala!*), a sense of wonder (*olé*), or even in a simple and ubiquitous greeting (*hola*).

Over the past hundred years or so, efforts have been made to 'de-Arabise' certain Spanish words and phrases when a clear Arabic possibility is available. One simple example can be found in the word *usted*, the Spanish formal 'you'. According to the official overseers of the language, based in their grand Royal Academy palace next to the Prado Museum in Madrid, *usted* derives from the archaic phrase *vuestra merced*, 'your mercy', along the lines of 'Your Highness' or 'Your Worship'. According to the theory, *vuestra merced* – which is quite a mouthful – is elided into *usted*, which then becomes the formal 'you'.

The explanation is plausible, and may possibly be correct. Yet it seems quite perverse to anyone with a smattering of Arabic, who, being aware of the near thousand-year presence of Arabic speakers in Spain, hears an almost exact replica of an Arabic term in the Spanish *usted*. This is the word generally transliterated as *ustadh*, but whose pronunciation is so similar to *usted* as to be practically indistinguishable. Literally, *ustadh* means 'master' or 'professor', but the term is regularly used in Arabic as an honorific, a means of showing respect to the person being spoken to – a necessary thing, perhaps, in a language which has no formal 'you', and therefore, like English, has to rely on shifts in register to achieve the desired effect.

Does the Spanish *usted*, then, come from *ustadh* or *vuestra merced*? These things may not be so black and white. Perhaps both, in some way, are involved in the forming of the word. What's important, however, is to acknowledge the possibility of an Arabic component.

The same principle applies to the word 'duende'. *Dueño de casa* may, at least in part, have a hand in its origins. But to claim that it is the sole source for the word denies, as with *usted*, a perfectly simple Arabic term which sounds very similar and with almost exactly the same meaning. This word is *djinn*.

Everyone is aware of the djinn through the *Arabian Nights*, where, in translation, these magical and frequently mischievous creatures have been anglicised as 'genies'. A djinn, according to the Qur'an, is a creature made of smokeless fire, a being invisible to the human eye, yet who lives beside us. Djinn are born, have families, and can exist in communities, much like humans. Some are good and others are bad; some like to interfere in human affairs while others remain aloof. Yet their existence, confirmed in the Islamic holy book, is never questioned. Humans and djinn coexist on earth, yet only one group – the djinn – can see the other.

'Djinn', therefore, has the same meaning as the principal definition given for 'duende', similar to the 'little people' present in folklore traditions throughout the world, and sometimes, though not entirely successfully, translated into English as 'goblin'. Duendes and *duendecillos* – little duendes – appear frequently in Spanish-language children's stories, much like elves or fairies or any manner of similar individuals in tales from almost all cultures. And they often inhabit and effectively control houses and buildings, much as they do in Scheherazade's magnificent compilation of tales.

Given the complete fit in meanings and the close similarity in sounds, it seems odd, then, to deny that the roots of the Spanish 'duende' lie, at least partially, in the Arabic 'djinn'. So here is an alternative theory regarding its etymology: that at some point during the highly dangerous period when the Inquisition imposed its cruel conformity on Spanish society (c. 1470s to 1830s), the phrase *'dueño de casa'* was concocted as a convenient and ostensibly Latin-based term by ordinary people desperate to disguise a deeply embedded and heretical belief in the existence of invisible beings as specified in the Qur'an, but not the Bible, and thereby save their skins. 'Djinn' – an Arabic word denoting an Islamic tradition – could easily have morphed among a largely illiterate population into *duen* or *dueño*, and hence into 'duende'.

It's a possibility, but almost impossible to know for certain.

This question is about much more than a slightly obscure point of word origins, however. Acknowledging the link between 'duende' and 'djinn' not only forms connections between Spanish, North African and Middle Eastern folklore traditions, but also helps to understand the many other layers of significance that duende has accrued. For beyond the realm of children's stories, the word has meanings and echoes so subtle and profound as to be almost indefinable.

But first, a very quick (and painless) lesson is necessary in Arabic grammar…

Almost all Arabic words are formed from roots made up of three consonants, a bit like building blocks.

Adding combinations of vowels, suffixes and prefixes to these three 'blocks' creates variants around a central theme or idea. For example, the consonants K, T and B carry the sense of 'writing'. From them you get the word *KiTaB* ('book'), *maKTuB* ('written'), *maKTaBa* (library), etc.

Many of these triconsonantal roots, however, have more than one central idea behind them, and in fact can have several, forming bunches of concepts all coalescing around a particular set of 'blocks'. This in turn creates groupings of ideas which at first glance may appear random, but which on reflection often carry poetic and other resonances, a fact exploited by writers of Arabic for centuries.

So, for example, the consonantal root H-B-B carries the sense both of 'love' (HuBB) and also 'seed' (HiBB). While A-Y-N gives the words for 'eye' as well as 'spring' or 'fountainhead'. (The ancient natural spring near where the Granadan poet Federico García Lorca was murdered in 1936 has the Arabic name *Ayn al-Dammar*, meaning both 'Spring of Tears' and 'Eye of Tears' – a curiously fitting name for the site of a tragic event that still resounds deeply in Spanish society and culture.)

Such are the extraordinary echoes and connections made by these groupings, that to delve into an Arabic dictionary can at times feel like opening up a codebook, laying bare a secret language of signifiers that speaks to us over hundreds and possibly thousands of years.

The root Gh-W-R, to give another example, carries meanings of 'running swiftly', a 'cleft in the ground', 'falling', and 'laurel bush'. All of which might seem unconnected until we remember the ancient Greek legend of Apollo taking over the Oracle at Delphi. When he did so, he chased after Daphne, daughter of Gaia, who ran away as fast she could. In order to save her daughter, Gaia opened up a cleft in the ground into which Daphne fell. At that very spot there was a laurel bush, and when Apollo reached it and saw that Daphne was now beyond his grasp, he was so enraged that he commanded that the laurel would henceforth belong to him, and crowned himself with it.

Curiously, all the meanings concentrated in the root Gh-W-R – 'swiftness', 'a cleft', 'falling', and 'laurel' – are key elements of this story…

But back to the word 'djinn', which is derived from the Arabic root J-N-N. Following what we have learned about the nature of Arabic words, the obvious step is to explore the concepts and ideas grouped around these particular consonants, or blocks. What can we decipher about 'djinn' from the code buried in the Arabic dictionary?

Well, along with its meaning as 'invisible spirit' or

'genie', the following ideas and words all come from the same three consonants:

- concealment, hiding, a veil
- nightfall, descending, falling
- madness, insanity, lunacy, obsession
- Paradise, a garden, the Garden of Eden
- ecstasy, rapture, possession
- daemonic
- protection, shelter, a shield
- heart, soul

Amazingly, the simple word 'djinn' – already a complex term in a contemporary, Western context given its simple meaning of 'spirit' – has multiple connotations which extend far beyond this, including both the heavenly and daemonic, the crazed and the secure, the bright lights of an ecstatic state of consciousness as well as the falling of darkness.

Even more remarkably, however, all these seemingly separate, distinct and even contradictory meanings are encompassed in the wider significance of the Spanish word 'duende'. And these are all explored over the course of this present book.

Duende is commonly associated with the art form of flamenco. Within flamenco circles it is rarely, if ever, talked of or mentioned, yet certain moments or experiences that flamenco spectacles can produce are known to have duende. They are not common, but exist nonetheless, and are the central key ingredient that sets flamenco apart from so many other forms of music. It is an experience that can only be felt, not explained – certainly not through words alone. But, simply put, it refers to certain states that flamenco can produce both in its performers and spectators where the veil separating the ordinary world from the extraordinary one momentarily falls, providing the briefest of glimpses of ineffable beauty, a beauty that can be ecstatic, transcendental or insanity-inducing depending on the person perceiving and experiencing it. When it happens it is unmistakable, yet trying to explain it to someone who has never tasted it is much like trying to describe colour to one born blind. Only the experience in itself will do.

Flamenco, however, does not have a monopoly on duende, nor does it claim one. The word can be used with its other, extra-dimensional meaning in non-flamenco contexts, including bullfighting. Yet the fact that it has become so closely associated with flamenco – that most iconic of Spanish musical forms – means that, to an extent, it has become trapped, as though it might only ever be used in certain Andalusian cultural contexts.

The truth is, however, that through its roots in the Arabic 'djinn', duende has a much greater reach, is in fact born out of a much vaster cultural context, and expresses a universal truth that can be perceived and understood by people all over the world in cultures quite different and distant from southern Spain.

Duende has a being, a substance, a reality which speaks directly to our essence, that part of us which is nonphysical and possibly eternal, in the sense of belonging to a realm of existence outside time: a quality traditionally referred to as the 'heart' or 'soul'. That it has been nurtured and expressed for so long in a relatively small corner of the globe – Andalusia – has perhaps given it a certain flavouring; the vehicle and the container have influenced each other. Yet the fact remains that those who can sense and feel it need not have one single drop of Andalusian or even Spanish blood running through their veins. What is required is a certain capacity, a sense, something capable of registering the invisible, the subtle, a power that is potentially both heavenly and daemonic, which can either enlighten you or send you mad. Or perhaps even both. No one can give you this sense, but it can, perhaps, be developed. Not least by becoming acquainted, or as acquainted as possible, with the concept of duende and it's many facets and dimensions, through the written word.

Go to a flamenco performance in Spain and you may expect to find the audience made up of a certain kind of person, a physical type, even, who attends such events. Rarely, however, will you ever come across such a diverse group, socially, racially, politically and distinct from one another in all manner of ways. Yet everyone present shares a common knowledge, a common understanding: a taste of the duende experience. You can see it in their eyes and it forms a bond: a shared belonging to a secret, invisible community.

FOUR STORIES

TRANSMISSION

For thousands of years, traditional folk stories in all corners of the world have acted as guardians of knowledge and wisdom. The 'poetic code' buried in the Arabic language links one word for 'story' with 'watering', 'irrigation', 'drinking', 'transmitting', and 'reflection', expressing an extraordinary truth about the role of the simple tale in fertilising both the individual mind and civilisation as a whole.

Stories that emerge from the Andaluso-Iberian context often contain elements pertinent to duende – overtly or otherwise – and can act as keys to unlocking a greater awareness of its needs and workings.

Here is a selection of some such tales.

THE PROPHECY AND THE LOCKED PALACE

At that time there was a palace in Toledo which had remained locked during the reigns of many previous Visigothic kings, barred to all. And each new monarch, on his coronation, had ordered for a new lock to be placed on the door.

When he became king, however, Rodrigo went against all advice and ordered that the palace be opened, hoping to find some great treasure hidden within.

But when the locks were finally broken, and he rushed inside to take a look, all Rodrigo could find there was a single, solitary chest. He ordered for it to be opened, and all that was found inside was a piece of cloth on which was written the following words:

Should the locks and bars ever be broken, and the palace and this chest be opened, let it be known that the people whose images are drawn on this cloth will invade Spain and subdue it.

When Rodrigo saw this, he was very sorry for what he had done and had the cloth placed back in the chest and the palace sealed once more. For the pictures on the cloth showed people in Arab dress, with turbans wrapped around their heads, seated on horses and wearing brightly coloured robes, with swords and bows in their hands and banners flying high.

And the king and his noblemen were much afraid.

From De rebus hispaniae, *Rodrigo Jiménez de Rada, 1243*

THE CALIPH AND THE GOATHERD

One morning the Caliph of Cordoba was out hunting when his horse was frightened by a snake and bolted, carrying his rider with him. The horse ran so fast that soon the Caliph's retinue was left far behind. Before too long, still galloping wildly, the horse came to a deep gorge and was just about to fall, taking the Caliph with him, when a goatherd – who happened to be there – leapt out and brought the horse under control at the edge of the precipice.

The Caliph was immensely grateful to the goatherd for saving his life, and in reward promised to make him happy, swearing on his beard that he would give him anything he asked.

The next day the goatherd went to the palace and was immediately granted an audience. His name was Ibn Adab, he told the caliph, and he had a herd of fifty goats. It would make him happy, he said, to have herd of a hundred goats, and so by his reckoning he would need fifty goats more. The Caliph listened and said:

'I see that you are content with very little, so, on top of the fifty new goats, you will also be given a little house to live in with a patch of land to feed your goats on.'

The goatherd was delighted, and left the palace thinking that now he really would be happy, because the Caliph had given him more than he had asked for, and that having a little house with some land would be very nice indeed. Soon he was settled in his new cottage and started to make friends with his neighbours.

Now one day an important neighbour came to see him, and told him that he had a larger house and two hundred goats, and a large tract of land with which to feed them.

That night the goatherd could barely sleep thinking about his neighbour's two hundred goats, and thought to himself: What a fool I was! Why didn't I think of asking the Caliph for two hundred goats? If I had, I would now be as grand and important as my neighbour.

And he kept thinking like this until he finally fell asleep with exhaustion.

The next morning, the goatherd presented himself at the palace gates and asked to see the Caliph, and once again was granted an audience. He told the Caliph about the night he had had and of the thoughts that had kept him awake. The caliph laughed on hearing his tale, and said that, as he had sworn on his beard to make him happy, he would give the goatherd what he wished for. And so he ordered that another hundred goats be given to him so that he would have a total of two hundred, just like his neighbour.

The goatherd went home as happy as anything. But, as soon as he walked through the door, he said to himself: 'So, because of his promise, if I had asked the Caliph for two hundred or even three hundred new goats, he would have given them to me! What a fool I am! As things stand, I only have two hundred goats now.'

He spent several days ruminating until finally he decided to return to the palace and tell the Caliph that he still wasn't happy and that he needed yet more goats and more land in order to feed them. When he did this, the Caliph repeated that he had taken an oath on his beard, and so gave Ibn Adab everything he asked for.

'I really am happy now,' thought the goatherd when he went home.

But his mood didn't last, for soon he began to think that even now what he had was not enough. And turning things over in his mind, he decided that he didn't want to live in the country any more but rather in the city, for life there seemed so much better.

And so it was that, as time passed, his little cottage was given over for a grand palace next to the Caliph's, and his goats were swapped for a collection of thoroughbred Arab horses, and the simple conversations he was used to with his neighbours became splendid parties and gala events where neither food nor drink were ever wanting.

The Caliph, meanwhile, was becoming increasingly irritated by the petitions and demands of the goatherd. Yet he had sworn by his beard to make him happy, and so he continued giving him anything he requested.

Ibn Adab, however, was never satisfied, and one day he appeared yet again before the Caliph.

'My Lord,' he said, 'you offered to make me happy and swore by your beard to give me anything I ask.'

'That is true,' sighed the Caliph, 'and if you have still not managed to find happiness, it will not be through any failing of mine.'

'Well in that case,' said the goatherd, 'what I need to be happy is to become Caliph. I want you to step aside. From now on I shall be in command.'

On hearing these words, the Caliph realised that there was only one thing he could do. He called for the Royal Barber to come at once. Then, in front of the entire court, he had his magnificent beard shaved off.

And when this was done he turned to the goatherd and said:

'Now I no longer have to keep the promise I made on my beard. And likewise, there is no reason for you not to go back to being what you once were.'

He ordered his servants to relieve Ibn Adab of everything he owned, of his palace and horses and wealth, and they returned him to where they had first found him: back in the countryside, on the edge of the precipice.

And there he remains to this day, just as he was on the morning he saved the Caliph, poor and lonely, with only his fifty goats to keep him company.

JULIANITA AND THE DUENDE

Every day, Julianita would ride on her mule, laden with heavy sacks of grain, to the spring in the sierra where cool mountain water formed a pool shaded by large, leafy chestnut trees.

Her parents were humble millers and had warned the girl time and again that she should not go there, for deep within those clear, crystal waters there was a secret magical power: it was known, in fact, to be none other than the home of a handsome and seductive duende. Many times had this duende been seen to appear as beautiful young women passed nearby, only to make them fall in love with him and whisk them away to his own world, never to be seen again.

The locals became so concerned about Julianita, in fact, that they used to sing a song about her:

> *Miller girl, miller girl, without any care,*
> *To the magical spring you must not turn,*
> *For as soon as the duende sees you there,*
> *On the path to your home you will never return.*

Julianita had heard these tales before, for they were common currency in the town, but she chose not to listen to them. Instead, every time she drew near the spring she felt an irresistible desire to get off her animal, step closer to the waters, and peer down at her own reflection in the bright clear stillness, lost in her thoughts and dreams.

Until one day…

It was an evening like any other, and Julianita was riding her mule along the path. Moments before, the sun had dipped over the horizon and the Evening Star shone brightly.

When they reached the spring, the mule stopped and Julianita got down and knelt over the waters to gaze at her own reflection there, as was her custom. But this time, to her great surprise, the waters were not clear at all, but quite disturbed. And the more she tried to see herself in them, the cloudier they became.

Then, all at once, the head and face of a charming and beautiful man appeared from the depths, gently rising through the water, and before Julianita knew what was happening, the man had stepped out and was standing beside her on the bank of the pool.

For a moment, fear gripped her, and she thought to run away. But it was no use, for the celestial expression in the man's eyes, seeming to glint with the light of the stars and the heavens themselves, captivated her. And all she could see before her, all she was aware of in the world, was this gallant and handsome prince, a man who now held his hands out tenderly and beckoned to her.

Gripped by a power greater than anything she had ever known, Julianita reached out her own hands towards him, and the instant their fingers touched, her heart and his were united as one, as though she had always known this man and had been waiting for this moment since her first breath.

Carefully and lovingly, the magical man lifted her up and, never ceasing to look deep into her eyes, slowly stepped back into the pool, sinking down into the water until both he and Julianita vanished into the depths. And no sooner had they disappeared than the waters returned to their normal, crystalline state.

As for the mule, when he realised that his mistress would not be returning, he slowly walked his own way back home, where his solitary appearance told the distraught miller and his wife everything they needed to know. They had lost their daughter to the duende; the words of the song had finally come true.

And from that moment to this, the spring has been known by everyone as '*la fuente de la Julianita*'.

THE KING AND THE MAGIC CARPET

The King of Seville's daughter was terribly ill, and after all the physicians in the land had tried and failed to heal her, the court magician was summoned.

'Cure the princess!' ordered the king. 'Or lose your head.'

The magician tried all manner of tricks and potions, but to no avail.

'Nothing can cure her, Majesty,' said the magician, trembling at the king's feet. 'She has been called to the invisible world; it is her time.'

'Nonsense!' cried the king. Yet as the poor magician was being dragged away, news arrived that the princess had indeed breathed her last.

For forty days the king locked himself in his rooms. After the death of his wife, his daughter had been his only joy. Now that she, too, had gone, all light had left his world.

On the day that his official mourning ended, he ordered the captain of the guard to come to him.

'Send your men out to every corner of the kingdom,' he said. 'Find every magician, every fakir, every wizard, every sorcerer and every person engaged in those nefarious arts, and throw them into gaol. And there they can rot while we decide what to do with them.'

The captain carried out his orders with great diligence: every practitioner of magic had their wands and other tools of sorcery seized and, powerless as a result, were cast in chains. Soon, not a single one was at liberty.

Years passed. The kingdom became known as the Land of No Magic. Most people's lives carried on much the same, but something subtle and important – something no one could quite put their finger on – was missing.

The king himself, however, was content.

'No more magic, no more misery,' he would say to himself every morning as he looked out from the palace window. 'Besides, they're all charlatans anyway.'

Now, with all the magicians incapacitated, there was nothing anyone could do to bring magic back. Yet in issuing his order, the king had missed one important category: magic carpets. These were still at large, if maintaining a low profile.

Yet realising that the fate of magic itself now rested with them, the carpets held an extraordinary assembly.

'Even our weavers have been imprisoned,' said the eldest when they all gathered in the shadow of a sacred, snow-capped mountain. 'If we do nothing, magic itself will cease to exist. There is only one thing for it: we must find the master weaver, he who created the very first of us. None other than Eight Fingers himself!'

'But where can we find him?' cried the assembled carpets. 'We don't even know what Eight Fingers looks like.'

'His whereabouts are unknown to anyone but himself,' said the ancient carpet. 'We must fly to every corner until we find him. For only he can restore order to the world.'

One of the carpets present was a young kilim, and with spirited determination he swore not to rest until Eight Fingers had been located.

Every night, when people at home were asleep, the carpet would set off into the starlit sky in search of the mysterious master.

But very soon the magic carpets themselves were in danger: sightings had been made of them as they crisscrossed the horizon on their quest, and in a rage, the king – believing he had eradicated all magic from his lands – ordered them to be hunted down. One by one the carpets were caught by the royal guards using nets, cannons, and all manner of means to bring them back to earth. And before long, the only magic carpet still evading capture was the young kilim.

'It's up to me!' it said, as it set off once more on its search.

High above the moonlit valley it soared, with the River Guadalquivir far below, stretched out like a silver ribbon. But that night the kilim, too, was spotted, and the captain of the royal guard sent up a new weapon – a flying machine – to capture it.

The kilim swooped and swerved in the air to escape, flying low to the ground in the hope that it might find somewhere to hide. Before long, it spied a cave in a mountainside. Diving into it as fast as it could, it tightened itself into a roll deep at the bottom.

The captain of the guard, however, was in pursuit, and sent a squadron of his best men to scour the landscape and bring the carpet to him.

Soon the soldiers were clambering over the rocks, and before long one of them had spotted the cave.

'Perhaps it's down there,' said the guard to his sergeant. Inside the cave, the kilim curled itself ever tighter, hoping against hope to remain unseen.

'Fool!' said the sergeant. 'Look, there's a spider's web covering the entrance. There's no way it's down there.'

The guard looked, and there, indeed, was a spider's web stretching unbroken from one side to the other. And so the soldiers moved on.

Deep in the cave, the kilim heard this, not believing its luck. And once it was safe to do so, it unrolled itself and peeped up towards the entrance. Lo and behold, it saw that there was indeed a large spider sitting at the middle of a great web covering the hole. And as a shaft of moonlight beamed down on it, the kilim saw the web transform into a rich tapestry of bright colours and designs, more beautiful than anything it had ever seen. The spider raised one leg as if to reveal itself, then another and another and another.

'One, two, three…' the kilim counted. '… Seven, eight. Eight fingers!' it cried. 'You are Eight Fingers! I have found you!'

The young kilim quickly told the master weaver everything that had happened, about the princess, the king, and the order against magic.

'I can help,' said Eight Fingers. 'But you must do exactly as I say.'

The kilim promised, and so the spider climbed onto its back, buried himself in its woollen fibres, and together they took off into the night sky.

Now the next night, in the Alcázar palace, the king was in his bedchamber getting ready to go to sleep when he looked down and saw a carpet by the bed.

'That's strange,' he said to himself. 'I don't remember seeing that there before.'

He was about to have it taken away when he thought that, actually, he rather liked it, that its colours and patterns were pleasing to him, and decided it should stay.

Just then, as he was standing on it, dressed only in his bed robes and about to pull back the sheets, the carpet rose into the air and as quick as a flash carried him out the open window and high above the city.

'Help!' cried the king. But they were so high up that no one could hear him.

Far into the night sky and over the distant horizon they flew. At first the king closed his eyes and curled into a ball, hoping it was just a nightmare. But every time he opened them, there he still was, on the carpet, soaring through the air as though it were the most natural thing in the world.

Clinging to the edge for dear life, he peered over and saw strange lands below, territories far beyond his own realms; mountains so tall that they touched the sky; lush green forests that stretched in every direction; vast oceans wider than his eyes could see, filled with amazing and monstrous creatures.

'No more!' cried the king, petrified with fear. 'No more!'

And with that, he woke up with a start, lying in his own bed, with the sun just beginning to rise.

Thank Heavens, he thought to himself. It was nothing but a dream.

The next night, however, when he was getting ready for bed, as he stepped on to the carpet the same thing happened again. Up it rose and out the window they flew. This time the king saw new wonders from on high: enormous cities inhabited by peoples he had never seen before, with magnificent temples and palaces far greater than his own. And although he was still frightened, and clung to the edge of the carpet until his knuckles went white, he gazed more intently at what he saw.

These people seem much happier than my own, he thought to himself. They are more prosperous and clearly love their ruler more than my people love me.

But before he could reflect any more, he found himself back in his bed, with the sun rising once more in the east.

On and on this continued every night. Directed by Eight Fingers, the kilim would transport the king to the distant corners of the earth, and on its travels showed him marvels far beyond his imagination. But the king also saw misery and suffering where it, too, was to be found. And he wept as powerfully as he rejoiced at the wonders before him.

Seven nights passed like this in which the king saw more than most people see in several lifetimes. On the eighth night, as he was getting ready for bed once more, he stood on the carpet and this time spoke to it.

'I know now that this is no dream,' he said. 'You are a magic carpet and I know that you have been transporting me to distant lands every night. Now it is my desire that you should carry me where *I* wish to go. Henceforth, you shall obey my commands!'

Instead, however, the carpet simply rose into the night air once more and whisked the king away. This time, rather than travelling to far horizons, it stayed within the Kingdom of Seville and visited, one by one, all the prisons where the magicians and wizards that had been locked up so many years before were still languishing, many of them now close to death.

And the king, confronted by the sight of them, grieved at what he had done, and wept more bitterly than before.

The next morning, when he woke up, he called for the captain of the guard and ordered the release of every man and woman who had been gaoled for practising magic.

'Henceforth,' an imperial decree declared, 'all magic carried out for the purposes of good is permitted. Magic is no longer forbidden.'

The people rejoiced and danced in the street at the news. And before long, as the magicians and sorcerers and witches came back to live among them, they noticed that something subtle and important –

something they couldn't quite put their finger on – had somehow returned to their lives.

And the king himself noticed it. He still mourned for his wife and daughter, but from now on did everything in his power to make sure his people could be as happy as possible.

As for the young kilim, well, the king went back to his chambers to look for it, but it had vanished. And they say that from that day on it has continued to fly with Eight Fingers to all four corners of the world, bringing a touch of magic back into the lives of those who most need it.

PROVERBS I

PROVERBS I

Traditional Spanish and Andalusian proverbs have emerged from a bedrock of wisdom stretching over a thousand years and are regularly used in ordinary conversation. Native speakers have such pride in them that once, when mentioning a British proverb to an elderly gentleman of Granada, I received the genuinely startled reply: 'You mean, the English have proverbs as well?'

We skim over these sayings at our own cost, for they often contain multiple layers of meaning which can reveal themselves the more we turn them over in our minds.

Half full

Those who cannot appreciate the good in life deserve nothing but disdain.

* * *

Silence

A fish dies through its mouth.

* * *

Danger

Sometimes the real hunter is the one who appears the least threatening.

* * *

Solitude

Better to be alone than in the wrong company.

* * *

Effort

You can't catch fish without getting wet.

* * *

Need

For a truly hungry person, there's no such thing as 'dry bread'.

* * *

Haste

Grapes ripen at their own pace.

Hypocrisy
A monkey dressed in silk is still a monkey.

* * *

Time
Sometimes the events of an entire year take place in a mere instant.

* * *

Envy
A thief believes everyone is the same as him.

* * *

Progress
You will die of old age and still be an apprentice.

* * *

Opportunity
Everyone makes firewood from a fallen tree.

* * *

Words

Better to remain silent than to bark like a dog.

* * *

Company

Tell me who you spend time with and I'll tell you who you are.

* * *

Struggle

God gives walnuts to eat to those with no teeth.

* * *

Surprise

A hare leaps out from where you least expect it.

* * *

Ingredients

Good wheat makes good bread.

* * *

Appearance

A monk isn't made by his habit.

* * *

Preparation
He who doesn't sow has no harvest.

* * *

Anticipation
He starts crying the moment he sees an onion.

* * *

Death
Neither fear it, nor seek it out.

ON DUENDE I

ON DUENDE I

The singer's name was Rosario. My wife and I had been granted access to her performance through a mutual friend, and afterwards we were introduced. She learned that my wife was a dancer and I a writer, and the three of us formed an immediate bond.

It turned out that she would be staying for a limited time very close to where we were living then, and so, in a very spontaneous and natural way, we ended up passing several weeks popping in and out of each other's homes, frequently unannounced, sharing many meals and holding long conversations as part of the Spanish ritual of the sobremesa, in which a perfect harmony is achieved between the act of sharing anecdotes, thoughts and feelings, and the act of digestion. These could easily stretch for nine or ten hours as lunch would flow seamlessly into dinner and beyond; Rosario would indulge her sweet tooth by creating delicious fruit-based puddings, washed down with *outrageously large glasses of brandy which she drank with near religious devotion in between long draws on her hand-rolled cigarettes.*

It was over the course of these times that she began to share her knowledge of duende. Duende was something that she lived by, something she breathed and in many ways — I realised later — even encapsulated. It was slightly strange at first: duende is something that is rarely, if ever, spoken about openly by those with a true knowledge of it. Yet it was as if, for this short period, a certain access had been granted and she felt free to express the inner reality of an experience that was as fundamental to her as the blood flowing through her veins.

After a few months, she moved on, continuing what we gathered was a peripatetic existence, but after only a few weeks we were shocked to hear of her death in a car accident. All at once, the evenings we had spent together and the knowledge she had passed on seemed to gain an added tragic weight and meaning.

Here is a selection of Rosario's comments, scribbled down in my notebooks — often in the early hours while they were still fresh. On the written page they can only partially convey the unique energy which accompanied them as they were spoken in her warm-toned, authoratative voice:

>Duende is a gift.
>>Duende is a harmonic.
>>Duende belongs to no one.

Duende is unobtainable.

* * *

Duende is something that you may or may not be worthy of receiving. You cannot know: the criteria behind it are beyond ordinary understanding.

* * *

Duende is experienced; it can never be explained.

The rational mind can come close to understanding duende, largely by dispensing with many of its assumptions and prerequisites. It can, however, never taste duende, which belongs to a different realm of existence, removed from the limitations of 'logic'.

At times, duende can appear to be an individual experience. In truth, it is always collective and universal, as it originates in, and belongs to, a harmony that exists beyond the parameters of the ordinary self.

* * *

A search for duende is almost always destined to failure if it is not understood that sheer willpower is not sufficient in itself, and may, in fact, become a barrier. Duende will find you – if you look for it correctly.

* * *

Duende experiences may have different, seemingly opposite, manifestations. They may be ecstatic, calm, fleeting, transformative, profound and shallow. They have led some people to change their lives completely, such can be the explosive nature of their force. Others may live with a near permanent and sustainable experience of duende in their everyday lives – a truth invisible to most other people. Despite an appearance of difference, however, the source of the experience is constant, and the same. What changes is the individual circumstances in each case, which give their own flavour to it – i.e. the characteristics of the vessel into which the liquid of the experience is poured.

* * *

Duende is a universal reality. It is most closely associated with flamenco, but in the Spanish-speaking world it can also be used in the context of bullfighting, traditional storytelling, poetry, art, music and children's playtime. Once its reality has been tasted and absorbed, it can consequently be perceived in non-Spanish cultures all over the world under many different names, often without ever having been given a name at all.

* * *

Duende is a reminder of our truer selves, the echo of something we once knew but have forgotten. The 'memory' it carries is the real nourishment it contains, and one experience of it may be all that we ever need.

* * *

Some animals have duende.

SILVER COWBELLS

SILVER COWBELLS

My first sustained experience of duende came from listening over and over to a certain song on a scratched vinyl recording of the great singer la Niña de los Peines. That track was called Esquilones de plata — *Silver Cowbells* — *and had a power about it that, for me at least, made it stand out from everything else on the disc. The lyrics are an adaptation by the singer — whose real name was Pastora Pavón — of a traditional Andalusian folk song collected by Federico García Lorca, which combined many of the elements that figured in his own writing: the pain of an impossible or unrequitable passion, and the ever-present threat of death. Lorca had a special admiration for la Niña de los Peines and the 'duende' experience that she was often able to produce through her art. She died in 1969 and is hailed as the greatest female flamenco singer of the 20th century.*

Silver cowbells, fine oxen:
The signs of a real man.

High on Palomares Hill
A labourer is ploughing with five
    poor workers.

You look at me from the corner
    of your eye,
Look me up and down;
Soon you'll see the wound I
    carry for loving you.

I threw a lemon high in the sky
And it stopped at your door:
Even the lemons know
We're in love.

Oh, what a mess!
The fun is over:
Now the shooting begins.

I climbed a green pine tree
To see if I could see him.
But all I could make out
Was dust from the car
Carrying him away.

WISDOM OF OLD GRANADA I

WISDOM OF OLD GRANADA I

In the early 1400s, a legal official in Islamic Granada began collecting and writing down examples of the rich oral traditions that he heard around him on a daily basis. Ibn Asim al-Gharnati's day job involved dealing with complex issues of religious jurisprudence, yet he was fascinated by the culture of ordinary people.

The anecdotes and sayings he gathered made up the bulk of a book he went on to publish called The Garden of Flowers, *a compendium of folk wisdom from the last kingdom of Al-Andalus, still holding out at that point against increasing pressure from the Christians to the north, yet only decades away from its final fall to Ferdinand and Isabella in 1492.*

It is interesting to note how familiar, and yet quite different, some of these sayings sound to the contemporary ear. They give a fascinating insight into daily life and attitudes in the last years of a culture that had thrived on the Iberian peninsula at that point for over 700 years, and from which the subtleties of duende continue to spread and penetrate into Spanish culture to this day.

It is impossible to speak the truth without lying.

* * *

If God wants to give you something, he knows the way to your house.

* * *

When the moon loves you, think no more of the stars.

* * *

If the path is right, do not concern yourself with how long it is.

* * *

The more you know, the more you lack.

* * *

What is the unknown? Something that hasn't been attempted.

* * *

What has your backside got to do with your heart, you ask?
The same blood flows through both.

* * *

The difference between a fool and a wise man is that only one of them knows his own shame.

* * *

Do not teach an orphan to cry.

* * *

Foolishness can only be cured through deceit.

* * *

Only children and fools speak the truth.

* * *

A thief isn't punished for his theft, but for his lack of skill.

* * *

A hawk doesn't hunt in the presence of an eagle.

* * *

Seek treasure in defeat.

* * *

Keep calling your donkey 'sir' until you get to the other side of the river.

* * *

Kiss her mouth and you will forget all others.

* * *

With the right signs, the question becomes unnecessary.

TWO GRANADAN WRITERS

FEDERICO GARCÍA LORCA

Much of the power of that lies in the poetry of Federico García Lorca derives from his almost unique sensitivity in early 20th-century Spain to the active element – essentially the 'treasure' – buried within the ancient local folklore of Andalusia. Thanks to his efforts, both the concept of duende and the duende-rich cante jondo *or 'deep song' within the flamenco tradition were given new life at a time when both popular and intellectual society were in danger of turning their backs on both. His success, however, came at a high price: his enlightened thinking made him the enemy of many involved in the military uprising in the summer of 1936 that led to the outbreak of the Spanish Civil War, and he was arrested, imprisoned and eventually shot alongside a school teacher and an anarchist bullfighter just outside the city of Granada.*

Here are a selection of Lorca's comments on duende:

Duende is a potency, not a finished piece of work; it is struggle, not thought.

* * *

There are neither maps nor disciplines to help us find duende.

* * *

The arrival of duende brings unknown feelings of freshness, a quality of something newly created – like a miracle.

* * *

Every art, and in fact every country, is capable of duende.

* * *

Everything that has black sounds has duende.
    (*Quoting flamenco* cantaor *Manuel Torre, d. 1933*)

IBN TUFAYL

Ibn Tufayl was a master polymath, thinker and writer born near Granada in 1105 in the town of Guadix, today the home of a large Spanish Gypsy community who live in caves carved into the sandstone hills surrounding the urban centre.

Ibn Tufayl was working at a time when many literate people in both the Islamic and Christian worlds were trying to reconcile a seeming contradiction between intuitive and rational thinking, between the truth as perceived through divine revelation (and subsequently written down in, and communicated through, holy books) and the truth as revealed through intellectual processes (as promoted by philosophers).

His answer was to write what is considered the first European novel, Hayy bin Yaqzan, *the Story of Alive Son of Awake, incidentally the originator of all desert-island tales written ever since. The book tells of a baby abandoned on an island and raised by a doe. As he grows up, Hayy – the protagonist* – develops his rational abilities through observation and analysis of the physical world around him, until he comes to a complete understanding of its workings. And it is then, when the training of his reasoning is complete, that intuitive and more revelatory capacities are awakened, culminating in his final vision of the true nature of reality.

As the pupil of Ibn Tufayl, the great Cordoban thinker Averroes later wrote: *'After the logical mind has been fully formed, it is necessary to move towards real philosophy.'*

The following is a passage from Ibn Tufayl's novel, where Hayy is trying to understand his first taste of an experience beyond the purely rational. In it he identifies certain key points relating to duende:

> He was now at a stage where, the moment he contemplated any object, he could discern within it traces of the force that had created it – the same force behind the creation of everything. So his thoughts therefore transferred immediately from 'the created' to focus instead on the force that was the source of all created things. This line of exploration continued in him until the longing he felt to know and understand this force became so intense that his heart detached from the world of the senses and attached itself to the higher world of thought and ideas alone.
>
> So it was that he attained knowledge of the permanent being whose existence has no cause, but

who is simultaneously the cause of all existence. And he asked himself how had he come to this understanding. Through which faculty had he acquired it?

He examined all his senses: hearing, sight, taste, smell and touch, and understood that each one of them could only register a physical object or what was inside a physical object. Hearing senses audibles: the waves created in the air when objects collide. Vision senses colour and light. Smell senses scent. Taste sense flavour, and touch senses the temper of things: their softness or hardness, their roughness or smoothness. Similarly, the imagination could only represent things that had physical dimensions of length, depth and breadth. Sensations are all related to the qualities of physical objects and the senses can detect nothing else. This is because the senses are powers dispersed within physical objects, and therefore as divided as they are divided. For this reason, the senses can only register parts of the whole, for if the power of sensing is dispersed over the fragments, it follows that whatever is sensed can only be a fragment as well.

It was now clear to him that the reality that he had experienced – of understanding the being which was the cause of all existence – could only be perceived by something non-physical, something that could not be a power within the physical body, nor associated with the physical in any way. And so he understood that the very thing that had given him this glimpse in the first place was the non-physical aspect of his own nature: namely, his essence.

But equally he saw that if someone were to have a taste of this experience and then not pursue it or do what was necessary to regain it, they would be caught in a state of extended suffering, a pain and longing from which they could only emerge after a great struggle.

And so he determined to concentrate on it, to not turn his back on it, until death took him in its grasp.

VIEWPOINTS

VIEWPOINTS

The following is a selection of quotes and aphorisms, all of which capture – from a multitude of different perspectives and cultures – an essence of duende:

Duende
    A mysterious power that everyone feels but that no philosopher has explained.

— GOETHE

* * *

The core
    My brain is only a receiver. In the universe there

is a core from which we obtain certain knowledge, strength, inspiration. I have not yet penetrated into the secrets of this core, but I know it exists.

— NIKOLA TESLA

* * *

Sanity

Too much sanity may be madness. And maddest of all to see life as it is, and not as it should be.

— CERVANTES

* * *

Poetry

I am on the poetic plane, where the yes and no of things is equally true.

— LORCA

* * *

Dance

    Cease, man, to mourn, to weep, to wail;
    Enjoy the shining hour of the sun;
    We dance along Death's icy brink,

But is the dance less full of fun?

— Sir Richard Burton

* * *

Experience
    Experience is not what happens to a man; it is what a man does with what happens to him.

— Aldous Huxley

* * *

Discovery
    Any life is made up of a single moment, the moment in which, once and for all, a man finds out who he is.

— Borges

* * *

Birth
    A single event can awaken within us a stranger totally unknown to us. To live is to be slowly born.

— Saint-Exupéry

* * *

Understanding

We understand more than we know.

— Pascal

* * *

Hearts and minds

Those who know their minds do not necessarily know their hearts.

— François de la Rochefoucauld

* * *

Struggle

All that was left was this anguished heart, eager to live, rebelling against the deadly order of the world that had been with him for forty years, and still struggling against the wall that separated him from the secret of all life, wanting to go further, to go beyond, and to discover, discover before dying, discover at last in order to be, just once to be, for a single second, but for ever.

— Camus

* * *

Truth

The truth is what it is, and continues to be the truth even though people think the opposite.

— Antonio Machado

* * *

Knowledge

The gulf between knowledge and truth is infinite.

— Henry Miller

* * *

Reason

It is never possible by pure reason to arrive at some absolute truth.

— Werner Heisenberg

* * *

Depth

It is easier to perceive error than to find truth, for

the former lies on the surface and is easily seen, while the latter lies in the depths, where few are willing to search for it.

— Goethe

* * *

Blood

When I'm singing well, my mouth tastes of blood.

— Camarón de la Isla

* * *

Illusion

No illusion is more stubbornly upheld than the sovereignty of the mind.

— Hans Magnus Enzensberger

* * *

Strange

'My dear fellow, said Sherlock Holmes as we sat on either side of the fire in his lodgings in Baker Street, 'life is infinitely stranger than anything which the mind of man could invent.'

— Sir Arthur Conan Doyle

* * *

Mystery

The truth about bullfighting is having a mystery to tell… and telling it.

— Rafael Gómez 'El Gallo'

* * *

Image

Everyone is as God made them – and often a great deal worse.

— Cervantes

* * *

Emptiness

Some hands achieve greatness by remaining empty; while others, clenched into fists, hold nothing.

— Ernestina de Campourcín

* * *

Slavery

The most degrading form of slavery is to be a slave to oneself.

— Seneca

Hate

To hate is to squander our hearts, and our hearts are the greatest treasure we have.

— Noel Clarasó

* * *

Unexpected

I never feel that any day has been lost; a lost day is simply a day with another agenda – the agenda of the unexpected.

— Luis Berlanga

* * *

Rules

There are no rules in art.

— Goya

* * *

Being

Every land you walked in was you, and you were never alone.

— Ibn Arabi

* * *

Science

I find it overly analytical, pretentious and superficial; largely because it doesn't take into account our dreams, the role of chance, laughter, feelings and paradoxes – all the things I love the most.

— Luis Buñuel

* * *

Answers

Asking questions is philosophy; finding answers is poetry.

— María Zambrano

* * *

Life

Until death takes us, all is life.

— Cervantes

TWO LYRICS

TWO LYRICS

In my *The Art of Flamenco*, I mentioned how the Pakistani qawwali singer Aziz Balouch found such powerful echoes between his music and the flamenco that he heard in Spain in the 1950s that he was able to perform on stage with Pepe Marchena, one of the flamenco greats of the time.

Likewise, the singer El Lebrijano, who died in 2016, regularly performed with Moroccan musicians who play a style called 'Andalusi' – a reference to its roots in Al-Andalus – insisting that there was essentially no difference between the two musical schools.

Here is further evidence demonstrating the partial Arabic roots of flamenco ('partial' because other musical styles, including Jewish, Gypsy and even Byzantine are among the elements included in the final cocktail that is flamenco).

It comes from the very close resemblance between two lyrics: one from an 18th-century Andalusi song, and the other from the Gypsy flamenco singer Antonio Mairena, who died in 1983. There is something very intense in the sentiment they both put across – and a truth based in the experience of duende. And while there is more formality in the Andalusi version, the connection is very obviously there.

First, here is the Andalusi lyric, taken from the collection put together by Muhammad al-Ha'ik in the 18th century, and translated from the Arabic:

> *Love may be just another part of life,*
> *but my heart fears its own*
> *passions.*
> *Where does it flutter to now, like a*
> *dove heading to the Strait?*
> *Ask yourselves, lovers: What are*
> *words? And what your secret*
> *thoughts?*
> *When they see me, they say: 'There*
> *goes the madman.*
> *'But leave him; he deserves his fate.*
> *Why did he fall in love in the first*
> *place?'*

And here is the second, sung by Antonio Mairena and translated from the Andalusian dialect:

> *Everyone who sees me on the street*
> *Is saying the same thing:*
> *'Falling in love*
> *Has sent that poor man mad.*
> *Pay him no attention:*
> *He lost his head,*
> *And has only himself to blame.'*

WISDOM OF OLD GRANADA II

WISDOM OF OLD GRANADA II

(*Collected by Ibn Asim al-Gharnati, early 15th century*)

Those who have a need walk blind.

* * *

Solomon's wedding party has finished, and now the beggars must return to their begging.

* * *

We cover her in perfume, yet still she smells.

* * *

Whatever the direction of the wind, use it to set sail.

* * *

War is easy for the spectators.

* * *

The value of something isn't known until it's lost.

* * *

What do you think? That there's blue paint behind the sky?

* * *

From drops of water are rivers formed.

* * *

Those who bring oil will find oil lamps.

* * *

The words of a friend make you cry, while those of an enemy make you laugh.

* * *

Everyone returns to where they came from.

* * *

Darkness of thought is not made brighter by a candle flame.

* * *

The darkness of night smothers our woes.

* * *

Better a pumpkin than a head with no guile.

* * *

Better a flushed face than a weary heart.

* * *

Heading towards Heaven in a roundabout way is better than going straight to Hell.

* * *

Such is the dove: white on the outside and black on the inside.

* * *

He sings of what is new.

* * *

Whether it's going to drink or not,
take the donkey to the water.

* * *

By the time the 'cure' arrives from Jerusalem,
the patient is already dead.

ON DUENDE II

ON DUENDE II

Sometimes duende comes from the earth, sometimes from the sky. Sometimes it comes from other people. Sometimes it comes – seemingly – from nothing. Such observations have an importance, but only at a secondary level.

* * *

Don't look for one: the duende experience *is* the message.

* * *

It is not necessary to express duende: that is a specific task for certain people. Try to become an expression of what duende is telling *you*.

You may not need duende. But if you do, it will find you whether you are looking for it or not.

Duende may find expression through artistic and other forms of creation. The expression exists that it may act as a vessel for duende, not the other way around.

* * *

Duende is spirit, breath, love, laughter and life. It can be felt as pain, passion, a passing madness – or in a thousand and one different ways. Many reject it or hide from it, preferring everyday sleep to the disquieting truths it can reveal.

Duende is not for the faint-hearted. To be faithful to duende may require a person to act against ordinary concepts of truth. Duende has – and is – its own truth. This is one of the reasons why over history many people involved in duende have appeared to be on the fringes of ordinary society, or to have had a playful attitude towards its rules and norms.

* * *

Although fundamentally different in nature to it, duende does not aim to abnegate or replace everyday experience; it adds to it and gives it greater extra dimensional substance, in the way that salt awakens and expands the flavours of a dish.

Duende is commonly thought of as being spontaneous and immediate. Yet it can equally act almost imperceptibly and over long periods of time, not least because it exists outside ordinary conceptions of time. Its fruits may be plucked and gorged on in one sitting, and often are. Yet this effectively kills the tree. Far better for it to be nurtured and returned to at irregular intervals. Then an understanding may emerge that the 'fruits' are only one element of more complex and dynamic whole.

* * *

At times it may be necessary to give up the search. In the space which is subsequently created, certain truths may be grasped.

* * *

Duende is work.

* * *

There is no set 'way of duende'. Duende has its own ways, which are imperceptible.

Duende is within you, yet it comes from without.

It is you, yet it is not you. To find it is to find yourself, yet 'yourself' is the barrier between you and it. This barrier cannot be 'overcome': it can only ever be understood.

Those who have duende are frequently unaware of the fact and would never claim to possess it in any way at all. This is not accidental.

THREE STORIES

THE GIRL AND THE MOORISH TREASURE

Once upon a time, there was a girl who lived at an inn on a main road. She was curious about everything, and was always being nosey.

One day a group of Moors arrived, carrying large chests with them. The girl was desperate to find out what the chests contained, so she decided to watch the men to find out what they were up to. After a while, the new guests went out for a stroll, and while they were gone the girl crept into their room. There, she opened the chests and discovered that they were stuffed to the brim with bright, shining treasure. Stunned, and not quite knowing what to do, the girl closed them again and tiptoed out.

Now, the Moors stayed at the inn for several days, as they had business in the area. One night, while everyone was asleep, the girl thought she heard footsteps downstairs and decided to go and investigate.

She saw that the noise was coming from none other than the Moorish guests, who were carrying their chests down into the cellar. The girl hid herself from view and watched: she saw how they lit a small candle and spoke a few words in Arabic. And as soon as they had done so, a wall in the cellar magically opened up.

The Moors crossed through the opening, hauling their treasure chests with them. Then they stepped out, extinguished the candle, and the opening in the wall closed again. At which point they returned to their room.

Now the girl was doubly intrigued, and started to wonder how she might get hold of the treasure for herself. So the next morning, she went and told the maidservant what she had seen. The two agreed that they should try to steal as much of the treasure as they could. And the following night, the maidservant slipped into the Moors' room as they were sleeping and managed to grab their candle.

The following morning, the Moors left the inn and continued on their journey. That very same night, the girl and the maidservant went down into the cellar. They stood in front of the same wall that the Moors had opened. And there, they lit the candle and the girl repeated the same Arabic words she had heard uttered two nights before. At that very moment, the wall opened up, and the girl stepped inside. But the maidservant, who was a little bit scared, remained where she was, tending the candle as best she could.

The girl was delighted to find the chests still bursting with treasure, and she started to fill a sack with as much as she could lay her hands on. But after a few minutes, the maidservant started to get nervous, and cried out:

'Hurry! The candle is almost going out.'

The girl, however, ignored her, trying to decide whether to take only the best pieces from the treasure, or all of it: it was all so shiny and tempting.

The maidservant called out again:

'Hurry! The candle is almost going out.'

Still trying to make up her mind, the girl hesitated, ignoring the maidservant.

'Hurry!' came the cry again. 'I can't keep it alight any more!'

And at that moment, the candle extinguished itself. Instantaneously, the wall closed, trapping the girl inside. The maidservant screamed and ran – up the stairs, out the main door, and along the road as fast as her legs could carry her, never daring to look back. No one ever saw her again.

As for the girl? Well, people relate how, from that day forward, strange cries and noises could be heard inside the inn, but no one could ever say where they came from. With time, a rumour spread that a spirit –

a duende – was trapped somewhere in the building and would wail and scream through the night. As time passed, and its reputation for being haunted spread, people started to avoid the place. And sometime later, the road itself was redirected and the inn was abandoned, left in the middle of the countryside with the girl still trapped inside. Until finally everyone forgot that it existed at all.

THE GOLDEN CLOAK

There once was a man who had a beautiful brightly coloured bird which used to sing the most exquisite songs. The bird was kept in a cage in a room which was always locked with seven keys, because no one in the entire world was permitted to see it. Not even the man's wife or his son were allowed into the room where the bird was kept. And of course, as they had heard of it, both his wife and his son wanted nothing more than to see it for themselves.

Now one day, the man had to leave the house and attend to matters which would keep him away for several hours. So, taking advantage of their opportunity, the wife and the son searched the man's clothes, digging deep into all his pockets until they found the seven keys which opened the forbidden room. Immediately they rushed to the door, unlocked it, and stepped inside. There they found the beautiful bird in its cage. They lifted it down, opened the cage, and took the bird out to admire it. But so smitten were they by its beauty that no sooner had they done so than the bird flew away.

Not long after, the father returned, and when he saw that his bird had escaped he became infuriated, so much so that he cursed his son:

'May you never be happy until you find the golden cloak!'

The next day, the poor boy, distraught at having been cursed by his own father, set out into the world to see if he could find the golden cloak. Before he left, his mother gave him a bag with three loaves of bread inside to eat along the way.

On the first day he ate the first loaf of bread, and when night fell he climbed a tree and fell asleep. The second day he ate the second loaf of bread, and on the third, the last, so that by the fourth day he had nothing left to eat, and decided to look for work. Along the way, he passed in front of a house where a mysterious little man was sitting on the step. The boy went up to him and asked if he could work for him, and the little man agreed.

'I won't make you work very hard,' he said. 'You'll just have to sweep and clean the house. In the pantry you will find plenty of food, so eat as much as you want, as it's all for you. You will have use of the whole house, except for that door at the end of the corridor, which you must, on no account, ever open. For if you do, woe betide you!'

At which point the little man disappeared.

The youth was conscientious and started cleaning the house immediately. When he had finished, he prepared himself a good meal, and when he could eat no more, went to bed and fell into a deep sleep.

So it was that the boy lived in the house for several weeks, cleaning it as the little man had asked, until one day, unable to resist his curiosity any more, he stepped purposefully to the end of the corridor. And there, forgetting everything he had been told, he reached out and pulled the handle of the forbidden door.

To his immense surprise, it opened up on to the most beautiful garden he had ever seen, stretching out to the far horizon, full of brightly coloured flowers, lush trees and extraordinary birds. He stepped into it to explore, and before too long came across a fountain where three beautiful maidens were busy washing clothes. Some of their items, he could see, had already been hung out to dry, and he noticed that one of these was none other than the golden cloak which he was desperately seeking. Without thinking twice, he ran up and pulled it off the line. But one of the girls saw him and grabbed the other end before he could get away. Meanwhile, the other two girls picked up the rest of their washing and fled.

Pulling with all their might, neither the youth nor the maiden let go of the cloak, until finally the young man spoke:

'Let me have the cloak,' he cried, 'for I have been cursed by my father and will never be happy until the golden cloak is mine. And now that I've found it, I cannot let it go.'

'If you want the cloak so much,' the young woman replied, 'you will have to marry me, because my life depends upon it.'

The young man was happy to agree to this proposal, for the girl was very pretty. And so without much ado, the two of them got married and headed back to the young man's home, carrying the golden cloak between them.

When they arrived, the boy's father was relieved to see that his son was now free of the curse. But the cloak was not only golden, it was enchanted, and outside the garden it was forbidden to be seen by anyone, otherwise the young woman would vanish into thin air. And so, as soon as the couple got inside the house, they hid the cloak as well as they could in case anybody should find it.

But the boy's mother was dying to look at the cloak that had brought so much luck and happiness to her son, and so she searched the house high and low until she found the box where the couple had hidden it. And no sooner had she opened it and seen the cloak than her daughter-in-law disappeared.

The son started looking for his wife, and when he couldn't find any sign of her he feared the worst. Meanwhile, his mother, who was becoming increasingly concerned, didn't dare tell him anything until, seeing how fraught he was, she finally confessed. The young man was deeply in love with his wife and decided that he would leave in search of her there and then, promising to find her no matter how long it took.

And so he set off once more, and wherever he went, and whoever he met, he asked if anybody had seen a girl carrying a golden cloak. But all along the way the answer was always no – nobody could give him news of his missing bride. Finally, after three years' searching in vain, he knocked on a door in the hope of finding a bed for the night.

Now in this house there lived a man who, instead of having hair on his body, was covered in feathers, for he was none other than the King of the Birds. He let the youth into his home and gave him shelter. The boy, in turn, told him about his search for his missing bride and asked his host if he had seen her. The King of the Birds answered that he had not seen a girl with a golden cloak, but wondered if his children might be able to help.

So he pulled out a flute, blew on it three times, and immediately all the birds in the world came to him, from the biggest to the smallest, and from the weakest to the strongest. And when they were all gathered, the King of the Birds asked them:

'Have any of you seen or heard of the mistress of the golden cloak, and do you know where we might find her? Let he who knows, speak up!'

All the birds shrugged and shook their heads, and said that they had heard nothing about this. Indeed, they began to wonder how it could be possible that none of them knew anything about the matter, until the Robin piped up and said:

'But not all of us are here. The Wren is missing, and he flies the highest. Perhaps he has seen something that we have not.'

When the King of the Birds saw that the Wren wasn't there, he became angry and ordered the Swift to fly out and find him. After a short while, the Swift returned with the poor Wren, who hadn't heard the King's call because water had got into his ears as he was washing himself. As soon as he was told about the youth's predicament, however, he said that he had indeed seen the girl with the golden cloak and knew exactly where she was.

The King ordered the Wren to take the youth to the girl, but as the bird was so small and couldn't carry him, he told the young man simply to follow the direction in which he flew. So it was that after seven days the Wren led the boy to a castle owned by a very powerful king, who was, in fact, the father of the girl with the golden cloak.

Standing outside the castle, the young man could see his wife at the window with a baby in her arms, and his heart was filled with joy. His wife spied him too, and the couple were delighted to be reunited. But immediately the girl told him to hide: her father should not see him on any account, for the truth was that he was furious with the youth for taking his daughter away and marrying her without his permission, and had sworn that if ever he were to find him, he would avenge himself by drinking his blood.

The young man was alarmed when he heard this, but his wife told him not to worry, that she would work out a way for her father to forgive him. And so, without anybody seeing, she managed to smuggle him inside the castle and hide him in a secret room.

The next day, the girl went to find her father and told him that she was missing her husband very much and wanted to see him again, not least so that he might meet their child. But when her father heard this, he became infuriated. The girl did what she could to calm him, but even when she managed to do so the King reminded her that he had sworn to drink the boy's blood, and that the word of a king was unbreakable.

The girl didn't give up, however. She wondered aloud if she might find a way to resolve this problem, and said that if she were to find her husband, perhaps she might make a small cut in his finger, collect the blood, and the King would then be able to drink it. In that way, nobody could say that he had not kept his word.

The King did not like the idea, but before he could refuse, his daughter told him that her husband was already in the castle and that they could carry out her plan immediately. She sent for the youth to be brought forward. The young man knelt meekly before his father-in-law and pleaded for forgiveness. Silently, the King took the young man's hand, quickly pulled out a knife and drew it across his finger. Then, lifting the cut to his mouth, he drank the boy's blood.

'Now I can forgive you,' he said.

And from that moment they all lived happily ever after. And, years later, when his bride's father died, the youth himself became King of that land.

ANGELINA AND THE LION

A wealthy landowner near Granada once had three beautiful daughters, each as lovely as the next. It was the man's custom to travel regularly through his lands to inspect them, but one day, as he was walking through a forest, a lion jumped out at him.

'I am hungry,' cried the Lion. 'And I'm going to eat you!'

In desperation, the man offered to go home and bring the Lion all the food he could carry if he would spare his life. The Lion had a think, and said:

'This is what we'll do: you go home, but instead of bringing me food, you will bring me the first thing you see as you approach your house.'

The man agreed and was most grateful to the beast.

'But if you do not keep your promise,' added the Lion, 'I shall seek you out and kill you.'

The man turned and rushed away. Despite his fright, his mind was easy because he assumed that the first thing he would see on arriving home would be his dog scampering out as usual to greet him. He would scoop the animal up and hurry back to the Lion without anyone seeing, for he knew that his daughters loved the dog very much.

With these thoughts in mind, he finally got home. But, oh misfortune! The first thing he saw on arriving was none other than his youngest daughter, Angelina. The man was so sad that he locked his daughter in her room. Soon after, however, his wife appeared and asked what was going on, and the man told her everything.

'Well, all you have to do,' said his wife, 'is take the dog. The Lion won't know the truth.'

The man thought this was a good idea, so he picked up the dog and went back with it into the forest.

There, the Lion was waiting for him, but no sooner had he arrived than the beast roared at him furiously:

'How dare you bring me your dog! Your daughter Angelina was the first thing you saw! Now hurry back and bring her to me or I will kill you.'

So the man went home again, even sadder than before, and he told his wife and his three daughters everything. The two eldest daughters said that they would never go into the forest and that their father should never hand Angelina over to the Lion. But Angelina herself said:

'If by going I can save my father's life, I will go, come what may.'

She said this with such firmness that her parents agreed, and so the father took her into the forest to where the Lion was waiting. And as soon as he saw Angelina, the Lion grabbed her and ran off to a cave, far from sight, leaving her father to weep as he trudged back home.

The Lion, meanwhile, carried Angelina deeper into the forest until they came to a great palace in a clearing.

'What a beautiful palace!' said Angelina. 'Who lives there?'

'Why, this is where I live,' said the Lion, 'and where you will live from now on.'

Angelina was delighted because the palace was beautiful and had everything she could ever need.

One day, Angelina was in her room when a little bird perched at her window and started looking at her intensely as if it wanted something. She asked the Lion what this meant, and he told her it was because the following day her elder sister was going to get married.

'May I go to the wedding?' asked Angelina.

'You can go,' said the Lion. 'Take the flying horse; you will be there in the blinking of an eye. But when you hear the horse calling, you must return immediately.'

Angelina promised, mounted the horse and, as the Lion had said, found herself at her parents house in less than a moment. There, she was greeted with much joy, for everyone was delighted to see that she was still alive. And she told them all about her new life.

She was able to spend a week with her family until, one morning, she heard the horse calling her. So she bade goodbye to her family, mounted the horse, and within an instant was back at the Lion's palace. And the Lion was very happy to see her back home.

Time passed, and one day, as Angelina was getting ready for bed, a little bird came to her window again. This time she could see that it had a broken wing and was in pain. Angelina sought out the Lion to ask what this meant, but the Lion didn't want to tell her. When she insisted, he finally relented and said:

'I'm sorry to say that it means your father has just died.'

Angelina began to weep and the Lion did all he could to comfort her. When she asked permission to go to her father's funeral, the Lion agreed with the same conditions as before.

'Take the flying horse,' he said, 'but when you hear it calling, you must come back immediately.'

Angelina flew back to her parents' house, where she arrived in time to accompany her father's body to the cemetery. She was so sad that she cried through the night, only falling asleep just as the sun was rising. For this reason, when the horse called her, she didn't hear.

When she awoke, she couldn't see the horse, and immediately understood what had happened. So she ran into the forest and went deeper and deeper until she found the path that led to the palace. But when she reached the clearing, the palace had disappeared and in its place was a pile of stones. She started to call out for the Lion but there was no reply. Finally, she seemed to hear his voice speaking to her from deep underground:

'Why do you seek me now?' he said. 'You have cast a spell on me for ever. Now leave me.'

But Angelina refused.

'What must I do to break the spell?' she asked.

'Buy some iron-soled shoes,' said the voice. 'And the day you wear them out, the spell will be broken.'

Angelina wondered how she might ever wear out a pair of shoes made of iron simply by walking about in them. Such a task seemed impossible. But then she remembered that soldiers spend their lives marching from one side of the country to another, so that might do the trick. And without further ado, she disguised herself as a man and enlisted in the army.

She became a member of the King's guard, and one day the King's son saw her and commented to his mother on her.

'I am convinced,' he said, 'that the soldier over there is a woman, for I have fallen in love with her.'

'Well if that is true,' said the Queen, 'go for a walk with her in the palace gardens. If she stops to pick the flowers, then she is obviously a girl.'

The Prince did as his mother said, and took the soldier for a walk in the gardens. But Angelina didn't pay the flowers any attention at all.

The Prince didn't give up, however, and insisted to his mother that the soldier in question was a woman, not a man. So the Queen said:

'Take her to the lake and ask her to go swimming with you. That way there will be no doubt about it.'

So the Prince returned to the soldier and asked her to go for a swim in the lake with him. But the soldier refused, saying that illness prevented her from swimming at that time.

Still refusing to be beaten, the Prince said:

'If you do not confess to me that you are a woman, I will tell my father the King that you have promised to kill the snake that lives in the sierra.'

Now everybody knew about the snake, which every day had to be fed one of the children from the kingdom as tribute, for it was ferocious and implacable and everyone lived in fear of it.

'As you say,' replied Angelina. 'I have made no such promise, but if the king orders me to do this, I will do it.'

The next day, the king called her and said:

'Is it true what they say, that you dare to take on the snake in the mountains?'

'I never said such a thing,' answered Angelina, 'but tomorrow morning I will take the place of the person destined for the snake and I will confront it.'

So Angelina prepared for her task, knowing that if she refused the King would have her killed.

As she was getting ready, a crow flew down and said:

'When you head off tomorrow to fight the snake, ask the King to give you a horse, a sharp sword, and a flask of wine. You should leave the wineskin open by the cave where the serpent lives, and when you see him appear and drink the wine, wait for him to have his fill and fall asleep, and then use the sword to cut off his head.'

Angelina followed the crow's advice and managed to kill the snake. Then she returned to the King carrying the serpent's head, and everybody in the kingdom celebrated her great triumph.

The Prince, however, did not give up, for he was even more convinced than before that this soldier was a woman and not a man, and he was falling even more in love with her. So once again he approached Angelina trying to get her to confess.

'If you don't tell me the truth,' he said, 'I will tell my father the King that you claim to be able to make the serpent's head speak. And if, when he calls you to perform this, you fail to do so, he will have you killed.'

'I never made that claim,' replied Angelina, 'but if I cannot make the serpent speak, I am willing to die.'

The Prince went to his father, and in less time than it takes to tell the King had called Angelina forward, and said:

'Is it true that you can make the head of the snake speak?'

'I don't know,' replied Angelina.

At this, the King got angry.

'Arrest him!' he cried. 'And take him to the dungeon. If, tomorrow, you do not make the snake's head speak in my presence, you will pay the highest penalty.'

Angelina was dragged away. That night, she was visited again by the crow, who perched outside the window bars.

'When they present you with the snake's head,' it said, 'call it three times and ask if it has reached the depths of the earth. If it says yes, beat the ground three times with your shoes.'

The next day, Angelina was presented with the serpent's head, and she could see that next to the executioner's block perched the crow. So she turned to the serpent and called out:

'Serpent! Serpent! Serpent!'

At once the snake's head replied:

'What do you want?'

'Tell me,' said Angelina, 'if you have managed to reach the depths of the earth.'

'Yes I have,' said the snake. 'I have been down here since you killed me.'

Angelina beat the ground three times with her iron shoes, and no sooner had she done so than they broke. In that instant the Lion, who Angelina still loved so much, magically appeared in front of the entire court. But he was no longer in the form of a Lion, but appeared now as a young, handsome, and beautifully dressed young man. Everyone was astonished to see him.

The man ran up to Angelina, took her in his arms and turned to the Prince:

'This soldier,' he said, 'is indeed a woman, just as you thought. But she is my wife, and not for you.'

And the couple leapt onto the flying horse and flew off to their palace in the woods, where they lived happily ever after.

TEN POEMS

TEN POEMS

The following verses, written by Andalusians during the period of Islamic domination of southern and eastern Spain, express qualities of duende both in their words and their intensity. Despite being many hundreds of years old, any one of them might form the lyrics sung today by contemporary flamenco cantaores.

HEARTFELT

I would slit my heart with a
    knife,
Place you inside,
And seal my chest
That you might live there –
    nowhere else –
Till Judgement Day:
So that you would be within me
    while I drew breath.
And on my death
You, too, would die with me,
Caught in the fabric of my
    heart,
In the darkness of my grave.

— Ibn Hazm

EXPLANATION

Just because my heart was
    moved
By a song
Doesn't mean I've betrayed my
    beliefs:
There is a time for seriousness
And a time for deep emotion.
For we are like branches from
    a tree
From which both the warrior's
    bow
And the singer's lute
Can be crafted.

— JUDGE IBRAHIM IBN UTHMAN

THE WINE DRINKER

'Give me your best,' I tell the
    cupbearer.
'Change my silver for the gold
    of your wine.'
And as I drown my sorrows in
    liquid
I watch the bubbles swim to the
    surface,
Looking like the whitened
    fingers
Of a hardened drinker,
Clinging for all eternity
To the bottle in his hand.

— Ubada ibn Ma al-Sama

YOUR VISIT

You came to me just before the ringing
Of the Christians' bells,
As a crescent moon rose into the sky
Like the white-haired eyebrow of an old man,
Or the delicate curve of the soles of your feet.
And although it was night, your coming
Made the arch of the horizon bright with colour,
Like the emblazoned fan of a peacock's tail.

— Ibn Hazm

THE WHEAT FIELD

See there the farmer's field
With heads of wheat
Pushed low by the wind:
Beaten cavalrymen in flight,
Bleeding from poppy-wounds.

— Judge Iyad

INSOMNIA

When the bird of sleep thought
    to make
Its nest in the pupil of my eye,
It noticed my eyelashes
And took fright,
Believing them to be
The bars of a cage.

— Abu ibn al-Hammara

THE DUNGEON

My prison cell is black and
    sombre like night,
Its outlines obscured,
Penetrating gloom at its heart.
And yet, outside, this black
    hole is
Bordered by flowers all white,
As blackest ink is held
In pots of palest ivory.

— Marwan ibn Abd al-Rahman

MOURNING IN AL-ANDALUS

If white is the colour of
    mourning in Al-Andalus,
This is how it should be.
Don't you see me?
I have dressed my hair
In the white of old age,
In mourning for my youth.

— Abu'l Hasan al-Husri

ABSENCE

I scan the heavens ceaselessly
In search of the star
That you are gazing at, too.
Every traveller I meet,
From every land,
I ask if they have smelt
The fragrance of you.
I turn my face towards
    every wind
In hope that its breeze might
Bring news of you;
Wandering, aimlessly
Down every road,
Reminded of your name
By every line of song.
And I stare,

Furtively, needlessly,
At the features of
Every one I pass,
Searching for a sign
Of the beauty of your face.

— Abu Bakr al-Turtusi

ON READING

My eye rescues
Prisoners from the page:
White to white
And black to black.

— Ibn Ammar

PROVERBS II

PROVERBS II

Collected from Spanish and Andalusian folk traditions:

Proportion
   Better to be the head of a mouse than the tail of a lion.

* * *

Expectation
   Don't expect pears to grow on an elm tree.

* * *

Patience
   Not all olives fall from the tree at once.

* * *

Service

Some take the chestnuts out of the fire, while others eat them.

* * *

Persistence

One flower does not make a garden.

* * *

Priorities

Do not cry over time already wasted, but over the time to come that you may yet lose.

* * *

Madness

Many lunatics started off thinking they were wise.

* * *

Treasure

Time is golden and life is a treasure.

* * *

Experience

In order to learn, you must lose.

The Pearl

Even though you can't see it, the pearl is in the shell.

* * *

Hope

Hope is the flower, not the fruit.

* * *

Repetition

Man is the only animal who trips up twice on the same stone.

* * *

Hospitality

Where there's enough food for three, there's enough for four.

* * *

Listen

Sometimes the dead can speak.

* * *

Sufficiency

If you've still got bread and lentils, what have you got to complain about?

* * *

Teaching

Those who speak, sow, and those who listen, gather the harvest.

* * *

Ignorance

A wise man understands that he knows nothing; only a fool thinks he knows.

* * *

Truth

The truth marries no one.

# BEING AND CONNECTION

BEING AND CONNECTION

Companion of my soul,
God has given you wisdom:
Just one word from you
Is worth two hundred of mine.

— Traditional Andalusian

The crystal streams
Are calling your name,
While the bells ringing
From the church tower
Merely whisper mine.

— Traditional Andalusian

ON DUENDE III

ON DUENDE III

To hear someone say 'So-and-so has duende', or 'So-and-so doesn't have duende' is almost always a sign that the person speaking is ignorant of what duende is and has had no genuine experience of its reality. There is no hope for them while they insist on viewing it in such an immature way.

* * *

Duende can exist in almost anything. Just because it can, however, doesn't necessarily mean that it does. The possibility for its perception lies within us because – in a manner of speaking – it *is* us. Yet it requires a certain quality, an activation. This activation, and the refinement of the perception of duende, are parts of the same whole.

*　*　*

Duende is the sun and you are the moon.

*　*　*

Duende is motion: it must flow. Try to trap it, to catch and retain it, and it will be lost to you. Try this too often and it may abandon you altogether.

*　*　*

Let there never be such a thing as a 'duendeologist'!

*　*　*

Flamenco has acted as a principal vehicle for duende for centuries. Duende was in existence before flamenco was formalised over the course of the 19th century, however, and behaves as a reality outside the sphere of flamenco in almost all human cultures around the world.

*　*　*

Duende is not anti-rational: it is simply that it cannot be grasped by the purely rational mind.

* * *

A person may act as a channel for duende and may help to produce experiences of it in others, yet be reprehensible in almost all other ways. This is confusing to some people, who imagine that roguishness is therefore a prerequisite for duende. It is not.

* * *

Speak of duende, and you may do more harm than good – both to others and yourself.

* * *

There is no 'recipe' for duende. The occasion, the company and the location may all appear to be 'aligned' yet fail to 'activate'. Duende is of itself: it cannot be called like an obedient dog.

* * *

There is no substitute for duende.

* * *

Some people get close to duende only to push it away, all the while imagining themselves to be moving forwards, even 'serving' or 'protecting' duende and its best interests. Their self-deception is often based on a persistent belief – a delusion – that the pursuit of duende is a form of self-embellishment.

* * *

Duende is a river: let it carry you to the sea.

* * *

You already have the pearl: just open your hand.

* * *

The obsessive search is no search at all.

Seek – the saying goes – and you shall find. Yet everything depends on the quality of the seeking in the first place. 'Wanting' and 'seeking' are not the same thing.

* * *

Duende can feel 'magical' and can at times appear to have magical qualities. And while it has certain affinities with it, it would be incorrect to equate it with magic. Magic is ultimately about power. Duende is about understanding – and release.

WISDOM OF OLD GRANADA III

WISDOM OF OLD GRANADA III

(Collected by Ibn Asim al-Gharnati, early 15th century)

Like a candle, that gives light to others while consuming itself in its own flame.

* * *

So if I'm a prince and you are too, who's going to drive the donkeys?

* * *

Give praise to the brave, even if they are your enemies.

* * *

Send your laziest child out to get the firewood.

* * *

God breaks your weaker leg.

* * *

When in prison, he prays; yet in the mosque, he whistles.

* * *

Waiting for the cakes to bake is better than eating them.

* * *

Mother goes out to do battle, while Father comes home to tell how it went.

* * *

We'll either die of thirst or walk on water.

* * *

Ask the patient, not the doctor.

* * *

It saw the cheese, but not the cat.

* * *

Accept the gift, even if it's no more than a bean.

* * *

Being brave is easy; leaving bravery behind is difficult.

THREE STORIES

ROSE VERDE AND THE CAPTAIN OF THE THIEVES

Once upon a time, there was a king whose only child was a young daughter. Every afternoon, the King and the Queen and the Princess would walk around the palace gardens for their daily exercise. One day, while on their walk, they met a Gypsy lady who offered to tell the princess's fortune. The King and Queen accepted with delight, but after the Gypsy had stared at the princess's hand, she told them in no uncertain terms that they must look after their daughter very carefully, for on her eighteenth birthday she was certain to be killed.

As the years passed, the King and Queen became more and more anxious about the Gypsy's prophecy. Finally, they became so worried that they decided to send the Princess to a castle in the middle of a forest, where she would be looked after by the housekeeper, who had a daughter of the same age.

The Princess was happy in her new home, and the years passed until her eighteenth birthday was only days away. One morning, as she leaned out of her window, she spied a cave not far away, from which four men were appearing. The Princess decided to go and investigate, so she found some rope, fastened it securely, and used it to climb down the castle walls. Then she set off in the direction of the cave.

As soon she found it, she went inside and saw a young boy there, cooking. It was clear from all the jewels and valuables lying around that the cave was used by thieves, and that the boy was the son of their captain. So the Princess hid and waited for the boy to leave, and as quickly as she could she threw the pot of food to the ground and scattered all the objects around the place, making a great mess. Then she ran as fast as she could back to her castle before anyone could see her.

When they returned, the thieves couldn't understand what had happened. So the next day, one of them stayed behind in case it should happen again. Meanwhile, back at the castle, the Princess told the daughter of the housekeeper about her adventure at the cave, and they decided to return together.

Soon after, the two girls arrived at the entrance of the cave, where the thief was waiting. He received them very graciously, and offered to show them inside. But the Princess was suspicious of the thief and his intentions, and said:

'We would love to. But first let's set the table and try some of that delicious-smelling stew that you have cooking over there.'

So the thief started setting the table, and while he was doing so, the two girls escaped and ran back to the castle.

When he heard about what had happened, the captain of the thieves decided that he would remain in the cave the following day himself. As he suspected, he soon received a visitor, this time the Princess on her own. The captain was very polite and hospitable towards her, and offered to show her inside the cave, including its deepest recesses, where they kept their most valuable treasures. But once again, the clever Princess was one step ahead.

'We can see it later,' she said, 'for now I would like to show you the castle where I live.'

The captain thought that this would be a very good opportunity to see inside the castle, a place that he would happily steal from at a future opportunity, so he agreed. When the two of them reached the castle walls, the Princess began to climb up the rope she had secured from her bedroom window. She told the captain of the thieves to follow behind her, but as soon as she reached the top, she grabbed a knife and cut the rope, sending the captain tumbling down. The captain was badly hurt and dragged himself back to the cave, swearing to avenge himself.

The next day, however, the Princess disguised herself as a doctor and called at the cave to offer her services. As their captain was so badly hurt, the thieves gratefully let her in. She asked to be left alone with the captain, at which point she started to beat him with nettles, leaving his skin red raw.

'Just you remember,' she said before leaving, 'my name is Rosa Verde, and don't you forget it!'

The Princess allowed a few days to pass, and then she disguised herself as a barber and returned to the cave to offer her services once more. As the captain hadn't moved from the cave for several days, his beard had grown quite long, so the thieves allowed her through. Left alone with the captain, the Princess spread foam on his chin and started shaving him roughly, leaving so many cuts on his face that it became a bloody mess. And as she left, she said:

'Just you remember, my name is Rosa Verde, and don't you forget it!'

A week later, it was the Princess's eighteenth birthday. The King and Queen arrived to fetch her and take her back to the palace, where they would surround her by guards. But at that moment, the captain of the thieves arrived disguised as a gentleman, and announced that he wished to marry the Princess.

The King and Queen called for their daughter, and she, recognising the captain instantly, agreed. So that very day the chaplain married the couple.

The Princess knew that the captain had returned seeking vengeance, so she ordered the palace cook to make for her a doll out of sweetmeats which would be an exact replica of herself. And on her wedding night, when the time came to go to bed, she lay the doll under the covers with strings tied to its head. With these, she could pull in one direction to make the doll nod, and in another direction to make it shake its head. Then she hid under the bed and waited.

Before long, the captain entered the bedchamber, locking the door behind him. He walked to the bed and spoke in a dark, ominous voice.

'Do you remember, Rosa Verde, how you threw our food around the cave?'

From under the bed, the Princess pulled the string to make the doll nod its head.

'And do you remember, Rosa Verde, how you made me fall from the castle walls?'

The doll nodded its head again.

'And do you remember, Rosa Verde, how you beat me with nettles?'

The doll nodded.

'And do you remember, Rosa Verde, the barber who ruined my face?'

For the fourth time, the doll nodded.

'Well now you are going to die!' the captain cried.

This time however, the doll shook its head. But the captain didn't see; in his rage, he pulled a dagger from his belt and plunged it into the heart of the doll, thinking it was the Princess. At that moment, however, a fountain of syrup spurted from the wound into the captain's face, staining his lips. The captain thought it was the Princess's blood but, tasting it, realised it was sweet. And he was instantly filled with remorse for what he had done.

'Oh Rosa Verde!' he cried. 'I had no idea you were so sweet and good! What have I done? Forgive me, Rosa Verde, for I have done a terrible thing.'

He was so distraught, and spoke with such sincerity, that the Princess appeared from under the bed and embraced him lovingly.

'You are my husband,' she said, 'and I will forgive you if you can forget what I did to you.'

The captain, amazed at what he was seeing, and delighted beyond words to see the Princess alive and well before him, immediately agreed. So the newlyweds embraced and made their peace.

And they lived happily ever after.

THE KING AND THE TRICKSTERS

Three tricksters went to see to a king, telling him they were weavers who could produce a strange and special kind of cloth that only a legitimate son of his father could see, and which no one else could, even if they thought they were legitimate.

Now the King liked the idea; with this cloth, he thought, he would be able to tell those who were really the sons of their supposed fathers and those who were not. So he ordered that a palace be set aside for the three men to make the cloth. To convince the King that they were genuine and sincere, the three tricksters agreed not to leave the building until the cloth had been made.

The weavers were given large amounts of gold, silver and silk and other things to work with. They set up their looms in the palace and pretended that they were working all day on the cloth.

After a few days, one of the tricksters went to the King and told him that they were making progress. And he asked the King to visit them – only that he should come alone.

The King was happy with this, but thought that he would get another opinion of the special cloth first, so he sent the Lord Chamberlain to have a look. The Lord Chamberlain duly went, but when he got there could see nothing. He dared not admit that the magical fabric was invisible to him for fear of exposing himself as a bastard, so he returned to the King and said that, yes, he had really seen it.

The King then sent another member of his retinue, and received the same report. So he decided to go and see for himself.

When he entered the palace, the King found the weavers there, who described the cloth in great detail, including its design. But the King could not see anything at all – for in truth there was no cloth. He began to feel very uneasy, fearing that he might not actually be the son of the King who was supposed to be his father.

'If *I* cannot see it,' he thought, 'I might lose my kingdom.' So instead he praised the cloth, and applauded the tricksters for their skill.

When he returned to his own palace, the King

continued to speak of the cloth as if it were real, although at the same time he suspected that something was wrong.

After a few days, the King asked his Wakil – the officer of justice – to go and see the cloth. Exactly the same thing happened to him: he went into the palace of the weavers, who described the pattern, though he could see nothing of any cloth of any kind. As with the King, the Wakil imagined that he was not the true son of his father, making the material invisible to him. Fearing that the discovery of this fact about him would mean the loss of his important position, he began to praise the non-existent cloth in even more extravagant terms than the King and the Lord Chamberlain.

The Wakil went back to the King, and told him that he had, indeed, viewed the cloth, and that it was the most extraordinary fabric in the world. The King was deeply distressed: there could now, he thought, be no doubt that he himself was not the son of the man he had thought was his father. But he nodded at the rapturous descriptions by the law officer. And he did not forget to add praise for the inspired workmen who were weaving it.

The King continued to send people to see the fabric, and likewise they all came back with the same impressions as everyone else.

Everything continued in this manner until the King was informed that the cloth was finished. He ordered a great feast to be prepared in which everyone should be dressed in clothes made from the magical material. So the tricksters arrived with 'a quantity of the cloth' rolled in fine linen, and asked the King how much would be needed. The King told them, and what kind of clothes were to be made.

The feast day arrived, and the clothes were said to be complete. The weavers came to the King with the magic robe which he himself was to wear. The King, of course, did not dare say that he could not see it, or even feel it.

Now the weavers pretended to dress the King in his new clothes, after which he mounted his horse and rode into the city. Luckily for him it was summer and the weather was warm. People who saw the King pass, however, were very surprised at what they saw. Yet word had already got around that only the illegitimate were unable to see the cloth, so everyone kept their amazement to themselves.

All of them except a black man who was among the crowds lining the streets. He immediately approached the King and said:

'Your Majesty, I do not care whose son I am. So I can tell you that in fact you are riding without any clothes on!'

At first the King hit the man, saying that he must be illegitimate and that was why the cloth was invisible to him. But other people, once the spell of silence and fear had been broken, saw that it was true, and started saying the same thing. At which point the King and his courtiers began to realise they had been tricked.

The alarm went out to catch the false weavers. But they, of course, had already fled, taking their generous payment with them.

(*From the* Conde Lucanor *by Don Juan Manuel, 14th century*)

THE LAMP WHO WENT IN SEARCH OF MAGIC

There once was a silversmith in Cordoba who made lamps. All day he made lamps, beating them into shape in his workshop before placing them on a shelf in the window for sale.

One day, the silversmith made a lamp which was just the same as all the others. But as the lamp waited to be sold, it said to itself: 'I am no ordinary lamp. I feel myself to be special, different. I have heard stories of extraordinary lamps that can do magical things. It is my strong desire to become one of them. In fact, I am convinced it is my destiny: I will become a magic lamp!'

It so happened that someone walked into the silversmith's shop at that very moment and picked the lamp up and bought it.

Aha! thought the lamp to itself. Here is proof that I

am special. Fate has set me on a path that will lead me to greatness. The way may be long and challenging, but I am more than up to the task, for a magic lamp I must become!

Everywhere it went, whenever it met others of its kind, the lamp would always ask the same question: 'How do I become a magic lamp? Please show me the way, for this is my life's goal.'

Now many lamps looked a bit askance when it said this. But others warmed to it.

'I, too, have heard of these famed magic lamps,' they would say. 'And I want to become one as well. We should stick together and create a brotherhood, for by combining our efforts we are bound to find a real magic lamp who can teach us its ways.'

Years passed like this, and the lamp travelled far and wide (for its owners were merchants who were frequently on the move). Often it was lucky in being able to journey in the company of its fellow seekers, and in all places they came to, whenever they met new lamps from different cultures and countries, they asked about how they might become magic lamps.

Finally, in a distant land, they met a shiny golden lamp encrusted with jewels who, when they approached with their usual question, answered: 'I am a magic lamp, and I can teach you how to become like me.'

At this, the lamp and its companions were

overjoyed. After so many years' searching, they were on the brink of fulfilling their destiny, for surely this magnificent lamp, whose shine and appearance had impressed them all the moment they had seen it, was the very one they had been dreaming of finding for so long, the one who would make their wishes come true.

'Our path to you has been long and arduous,' they all cried. 'And we are so keen to learn! When can we start?'

'Soon,' promised the golden lamp. 'But first, I have become a little tarnished while I have been here waiting for you to find me; you must clean me.'

'Of course,' the lamps eagerly replied. 'And could you show us some magic?'

'All in good time,' said the golden lamp.

The cleaning process seemed to last an age – far longer than any of them expected. When they had finished, they turned to the golden lamp and said: 'Now can you teach us?'

'Later,' the golden lamp said. 'For now, I want you to find new jewels to decorate me. You see how one or two of them have been lost over the years? In order to teach you, I myself must first be complete. Now off you go and find them for me.'

The other lamps were impressed by the great teacher's humility in showing its imperfections, and their belief in it was strengthened even further as they set off on their quest.

'When we return with the jewels, then it will display its powers to us, and will show us the way to become magic lamps ourselves,' they confided to one another.

The search for the jewels took even longer than the first task, yet finally, after many trials, the gems were secured and brought back to the golden lamp.

'Now can we learn your secrets?' the lamps eagerly asked.

'You are too impatient!' cried the golden lamp. 'And your impatience makes you unworthy.'

The lamps bowed their heads in shame.

'You have brought me new jewels,' the golden lamp continued, 'but they need to be set into my sides. Only then will I be complete.'

The student lamps were humbled by its wisdom, and embarked on their new task. It was very difficult for them, and required much training and effort on their part, but eventually, after yet more time had passed, they were able to begin. The lamp of our story was given the job of placing a gem on the master lamp's lid. Yet as it got closer, it noticed something: a tiny chip on the lamp's side revealed a dull metal colour beneath where the gilt had gone. Scratching a little more, it realised that the whole of the 'golden' lamp was in fact the same.

All at once, the lamp's head began to spin as it realised that the 'master lamp' was no master at all. It wasn't even made of gold, for underneath the shiny exterior it was, in fact, made of nothing more than ordinary copper.

'You are no magic lamp,' it cried. 'You are a fraud!'

Distraught and confused, the lamp left the company of its fellow seekers and wandered off alone. For many years it was just another solitary household item with no sense of purpose in life. So great was its disappointment that it lost all faith: in itself, in magic, even in being alive.

Meanwhile, after so many years' trying to learn magic, and now cast into a pit of despondency, it had practically forgotten to do the one thing it had been made for: to give people light. The truth was that it had been getting steadily worse at this one simple task for many years, and had passed from one owner to another, its value dropping each time, until finally it woke up one day to find itself back at the silversmith's in Cordoba where its journey had begun so long before, cast on to a pile of old, almost useless lamps destined for smelting down.

'Oh, woe is me!' cried the lamp. 'After such high hopes and such great beginnings, not only have I been deceived and betrayed, yet here I am, cast on to the heap of failure. My dream of becoming a magic lamp was nothing but a nightmare that has brought me to the sorriest of endings. I am nothing.'

At this, an elderly and tarnished old lamp on the shelf spoke.

'What is this talk of *magic* lamps?' it said. 'You are a lamp, and a lamp alone. What made you think that there was such a thing as a magic lamp? Or that you might even become one?'

The lamp looked up, and recognised the old lamp who was speaking.

'But you,' it cried, 'were the one who told me stories of magic lamps in the first place. It was *you* who told those tales that set me off on my quest.'

'Perhaps,' said the old lamp, 'you need to hear them again.'

And so it began to tell the stories that the lamp had heard it recite so many years before: tales of kings and queens, of duendes and fairies, of magicians and witches, and of djinns and genies – some of whom, at times, could be coaxed out of ordinary oil lamps. At first the lamp refused to listen; the stories were, after all, the cause of all its misfortune. But the storyteller persisted, and as it repeated its tales, the lamp began to pay attention, more closely, until finally, after much time had passed, it felt that it knew them all and could retell them itself.

And on the day that the meaning of the stories finally became clear to the lamp, the silversmith leant down and picked it up from the pile, gave it a clean, and put it out for sale once more.

Today, now that it has stopped wanting to be something it can never become, the lamp is steadily getting better at doing what it was always meant to do: provide people with light.

As for the question of magic, it leaves that to others.

But is there magic to be found *inside* the lamp, you ask?

That is a very different question.

And the only answer is to rub it… and find out.

ON DUENDE IV

ON DUENDE IV

Because duende doesn't understand time in the ordinary sense, it may provoke perceptions which appear to be 'ahead of themselves'. Others can reveal previously unknown truths about 'past' events. Within the duende experience, temporal definitions lose their ordinary significance.

* * *

When the doors open, previous steps lose all importance and effectively vanish.

* * *

If you want a firework display, look elsewhere.

* * *

The form that duende takes emerges out of a dynamic relationship between the substance of duende itself and the person or people acting as a channel for its expression. It is not form alone. Those who look at past practitioners of duende and then expect those of the present and future to ape them haven't grasped this truth. Duende is constant, but the outward means for its expression are in constant flux.

When duende is expressed through you, or through your creation, you gain nothing. Any 'gain' is exclusively for others capable of perceiving and receiving it.

* * *

The motions of duende – how and when it comes and goes – are entirely the concern of duende itself. All a person can do is prepare themselves to receive it. Part of that preparation is observing duende operating through others.

What duende actually is lies beyond ordinary understanding. No verbal definition of it can ever suffice because words alone cannot describe it. At best, words can help to prepare someone for an experience of duende, and can – on very rare occasions – provoke an experience of it in themselves. Historically, some forms of poetry have been a medium for this.

* * *

'What is duende?' is almost always the wrong question, followed by 'Where can I find it?' Part of the problem lies in the idea that it is necessarily something that lies 'out *there*'.

* * *

Refinement of the perception of duende is continuous and perpetual. There is no 'end point', no moment of 'arriving'. Any sensation along those lines is at best a signal of beginning – and often of a stage before that.

* * *

Duende cannot – and does not – exist in isolation. It is not a single note. A great number of elements are integral to it, including many different facets of the individuality – seemingly unconnected and often previously 'hidden' or under-explored. Added to these are factors which lie outside the ordinary constraints of the self, including a direct form of communication with others. This communication is entirely telepathic.

* * *

Your 'self' is both what separates you from duende and the vehicle you must use to find it.

There may be long periods in life where duende appears to be absent, unobtainable, perhaps gone for good. Often this is because duende itself needs you to be working on something – either in yourself or with others: something which in turn enables a greater and more subtle perception of duende when it 'returns'. The truth is that it is never absent. Only our perception of it wavers – sometimes by necessity.

* * *

'Produce duende!' is the command of a fool.

* * *

There can be duende without understanding. But there can be no understanding without duende.

EPILOGUE

Often what we are looking for is staring us in the face, perhaps for years or even decades, without our even seeing it.

Shortly after finishing my first book, *Duende*, I embarked upon my second, *Andalus: Unlocking the Secrets of Moorish Spain*, in an attempt to explore the often-overlooked legacy from the Islamic period in Spanish history. During my research, I was struck how the same folk tale, in varying guises, cropped up again and again in both Spain and Portugal. The story always involved 'Moors' leaving behind a treasure, often magically secreted in a cave or buried beneath a tree as they retreated in the face of Christian advance, and then a girl – frequently a Moorish king's daughter – left behind to guard it. In the story of The Girl and the Moorish Treasure, told earlier in this book, this structure is given an interesting twist in that the Moors are passing travellers, and the 'girl' is trying to steal their treasure rather than protect it. The fundamental elements, however – Moors, magic, treasure, and a girl – are all there.

For a long time I felt as though these tales held an important clue to understanding something of the power that Spain had over me, for I have been spellbound to varying degrees by the country since I first encountered it, through images of the Alhambra, when I was in my teens. I was tantalised by a sense that out there, somewhere, there was a kind of 'treasure' that had been introduced to the Iberian peninsula and embedded in it, possibly during the period of Al-Andalus. Yet I could never quite find it, or put my finger on what it might be. It seemed to be some kind of magical power, perhaps: a sense, a feeling, a possibility: something that you knew existed because you felt it, if only vaguely at times, yet which defied all efforts at being discovered. The more I searched, the more it eluded me – or appeared to – and so all I could do was hint at it, like a pot of gold at the end of the rainbow that can never, in truth, be found...

Only many years later, when I had effectively forgotten this quest and written about dozens of other aspects of Spanish life and culture, did I understand that in fact I had known what the 'treasure' was all along, before I had come across the many stories that spoke of its existence. Not only that, I had even written about it, using the Spanish word for it as the title of my first book. It was, of course, nothing less than 'duende' itself, but rather than realising this, I had fallen into the trap of thinking that what I was seeking must be 'something else', something 'out there', and effectively blinded myself to the pearl that was already sitting in my hand.

Part of the problem also lay in the fact that at that point I still thought of duende as something exclusive to Andalusia, and flamenco in particular. Although I had searched for it and experienced it, my understanding of it was still quite limited; I had yet to appreciate the universality of it, perceive it as something that was closely bound with flamenco but which had an existence beyond it as well: musical expression was one way into duende, but not the only way, as I later realised.

As the Spanish saying goes, 'In order to learn, you have to lose', and in my case what needed to be lost were certain preconceived ideas about what duende is, its source, and what it is capable of. Only when these had been shaken – helped by 'losses' in my own personal circumstances – did a new comprehension of duende begin to open up.

This then, is the essence of a truth alluded to obliquely through the course of this book, but stated clearly here:

. . .

Duende is an active, subtle ingredient, parallel to the concepts surrounding the Arabic word 'djinn', which was injected into Iberian culture at some time over the past thousand years or more, probably through contact with the Middle East facilitated by Spain's absorption into the Islamic Empire from the early 8th century. It both nourished and was expressed through several art forms practised by Muslims, Christians, Jews and Gypsies over the centuries – notably poetry, literature, music and painting until, somewhere around the end of the 18th and early 19th centuries, it became strongly associated with flamenco, which was emerging in Andalusia at the time into the form that we know it as today. From then until now, it has been almost inextricably bound with flamenco music and dance, although figures such as Goethe and Lorca have hinted at its wider scope. Other, more recent artists and commentators, however, have begun to speak about duende more frequently as something connected, but not exclusive to, flamenco, and it appears that after some two hundred years, duende can now be understood and appreciated as a quality that extends far beyond the boundaries of modern Andalusia, and which has an importance, perhaps, for everyone throughout the world.

. . .

In the normal course of things, this kind of statement would be made at the start of a book: a setting out of one's stall in the hope that the reader may be drawn in and tempted to carry on reading. But, in my still-limited understanding, duende itself rarely, if at all, operates in a 'normal' way and can often appear upside down or back to front in comparison to our everyday assumptions. And so, in honour of this, I place it here, in the epilogue, at the end.

Unless, of course, this is merely a beginning…

ACKNOWLEDGMENTS

My thanks to Spike Golding for his design genius, and to Sian Phillips for proofreading.

The following have signed up to my Patreon page (patreon.com/jasonwebsterwriter), and thereby provided a huge contribution to the creation of this book. My sincere thanks to you all: Duke Tate, Margie Savory, Roger Buglass, Ian Mitchell, Frederick Sleap, Kifah Arif, Anna Yakovenko, Jules Stewart, Rob Sheardown, Karole Webster, Miles Roddis, Ulrika Eriksson, Nigel Wheatley, Peter Davies, Randy Villines, Luke Baxter, John Webster, Juliette Wright, Neville Austin, Alan Williams, Jane Richardson, and Mark Blandford.

And lastly, as ever, my thanks to Salud, Arturo and Gabi.

REQUEST

Good reviews are a great help

If you enjoyed this book, please review it on **Amazon**, **Goodreads**, or anywhere else you prefer.

Thank you.

The Corsario team